Freethought and Freedom

Freethought and Freedom

THE ESSAYS OF
GEORGE H. SMITH

CATO INSTITUTE
WASHINGTON, D.C.

eBook ISBN: 978-1-944424-38-1
Print ISBN: 978-1-944424-37-4

Library of Congress Cataloging-in-Publication Data available.

Printed in the United States of America.

CATO INSTITUTE
1000 Massachusetts Avenue, N.W.
Washington, D.C. 20001
www.cato.org

CONTENTS

1

Augustine's Case for Righteous Persecution

One thing that united nearly all early freethinkers was their consistent opposition to religious persecution, or to any state interference in religious beliefs and practices that are peaceful. (One notable exception was Thomas Hobbes, who wished the state to control religious practices; but those freethinkers who relied upon Hobbes's criticisms of the Bible and other matters relating to Christianity typically repudiated his political absolutism.) Most freethinkers from the late 17th century through the 19th century were tireless advocates not merely of religious toleration but of complete religious freedom, including freedom for Jews and atheists. Additionally, freethinkers in Catholic countries called for freedom for Protestants, while freethinkers in Protestant countries defended freedom for Catholics.

The history of religious persecution in Christendom is complicated, but leading theologians, both Catholic and Protestant (Augustine, Aquinas, Luther, Calvin, etc.), defended it passionately with extensive arguments. Thus, if we are to appreciate what the freethinkers were up against and how they crafted their pro-freedom arguments, we must know something about the arguments they sought to overthrow. The purpose of this essay (and the one that follows) is to sketch some of the main pro-persecution arguments. For more details, I recommend the excellent overview by Perez Zagorin, *How the Idea of Religious Toleration Came to the West* (Princeton University Press, 2005); and the magisterial two-volume work by the Catholic historian Joseph Lecler, *Toleration and the Reformation* (Longmans, English translation 1960).

Although Christians were a small minority in the Roman Empire and were sporadic victims of state persecution, some leading Christian apologists defended religious freedom. One of the best was Tertullian (c. 145–225), a lawyer and former pagan who converted to Christianity late in life (and who would himself be condemned as a heretic). Tertullian wrote:

> It is a fundamental human right, a privilege of nature, that every man should worship according to his own

convictions: one man's religion neither harms nor helps another man. It is assuredly no part of religion—to which free will and not force should lead us.

A later apologist, Lactantius (c. 240–320), argued that religious beliefs cannot be meritorious unless they are accepted freely—a theme that would reverberate for many centuries in the arguments for toleration.

> If you wish to defend religion by bloodshed, and by tortures, and by guilt, it will no longer be defended, but will be polluted and profaned. For nothing is so much a matter of free-will as religion; in which, if the mind of the worshipper is disinclined to it, religion is at once taken away, and ceases to exist.

Lactantius dismissed a rationale for persecution that, ironically, would later be used by Augustine to defend persecution by Christians. Perhaps the beneficiaries of persecution are the victims themselves. Perhaps Christians benefit in the long run when they are compelled to sacrifice to the pagan gods. The response of Lactantius to this "for their own good" argument was brief but suggestive: "that is not a kindness which is done to one who refuses it." True concern for the welfare of others is never manifested in violence or threats of violence.

Lactantius considered another justification for Roman persecution: that it served the pagan gods who rightfully demanded sacrifices as tokens of loyalty, gratitude, and esteem. (Again, this argument, appropriately modified, would later become a mainstay of Christian persecutors, especially Calvinists.) According to Lactantius, however, "that is not a sacrifice which is extorted from a person against his will." Unless a sacrifice is offered "spontaneously" and "from the soul," it is nothing more than a "curse" extracted "by injuries, by prison, by tortures."

Perhaps the most interesting argument by Lactantius is one that would be invoked repeatedly by later freethinkers. Suppose a god really does demand worship by violent means. Any such god, Lactantius retorted, would be unworthy of our worship. Cruel gods "are doubtless worthy of the detestation of men, since libations are made to them with tears, with groaning, and with blood flowing from all the limbs."

In 313, the Edict of Milan (issued jointly by Constantine and Licinius) established religious liberty as a fundamental principle of public law. Before long, however, the emperor Constantine was bestowing special favors on the Christian church. His Christian successors continued the policy until Theodosius revoked the Edict of Milan during his despotic reign (379–395). Theodosius established orthodox

Christianity as the official religion, outlawed pagan worship and rituals, and decreed severe penalties for heresy.

Thus did a religion born in opposition to the state become its friend and ally. As the classical liberal and Catholic historian Lord Acton put it, "Christianity, which in earlier times had addressed itself to the masses, and relied on the principle of liberty, now made its appeal to the rulers, and threw its mighty influence into the scale of authority."

Since the hare is more likely than the hound to oppose blood sports, it is perhaps understandable that the number of Christian defenders of religious freedom declined precipitously after Christians gained control of the reins of state power. Indeed, it was left to the perverse genius of St. Augustine (354–430) to develop the first systematic defense of religious persecution in the history of Western civilization. Augustine called his approach "righteous persecution" because it justified persecution for the righteous cause of saving people from the eternal torments of hell. That was essentially a variant of the "for their own good" argument that Lactantius had rebutted previously, and it would remain a powerful and popular argument for many centuries.

Augustine started out as an eloquent defender of religious toleration, but he changed his mind after becoming embroiled in a bitter and sometimes violent conflict (in North Africa) with a large group of Christian schismatics known as Donatists. Augustine's initial case for toleration was based largely on the fact that beliefs, per se, cannot be compelled. "No one can or ought to be constrained to believe," according to the early Augustine. The mind cannot be forced to believe a doctrine; only arguments, evidence, or internal events (such as a flash of inspiration) can cause us to believe something, so coercion is *useless* in matters of religion. That argument, which became a standard refrain in later arguments for toleration— we find it in the Levellers and in John Locke, for example— might seem impossible to overcome. But Augustine was an ingenious fellow. After becoming a champion of persecution, Augustine replied to his own early argument by pointing out that empirical evidence did not support the theoretical claim that coercion is impotent in matters of belief. After all, there were many instances of heretics who had been "brought over to the Catholic unity by fear."

Clearly, persecution had worked in those cases, but how? Augustine still denied that beliefs, per se, can be compelled, at least directly. But the threat of force *can* break "the heavy chains of inveterate custom." Some heretics were "too listless, or conceited, or sluggish, to take pains to examine Catholic truth." Others feared reprisals from fellow heretics. Others were raised as heretics and never knew any better. Others planned to embrace orthodoxy eventually but were afflicted with procrastination. In such cases, according to Augustine, persecution, though unable to compel belief, can and often does change the heretic's mental attitude by breaking the bonds of bad habits, indifference, and sloth. Thus, even if coercion cannot impart truth, it can *prepare* the heretic to hear and receive the truth. The fear of punishment cannot change a person's beliefs directly, but it can influence them *indirectly* by softening up the heretic, so to speak.

Even if we grant that coercion can affect beliefs, *why* should Christians use force or the threat of force against heretics and others who do not subscribe to the tenets of orthodox Christianity? Here, Augustine presented the interesting hypothetical of a house that we know "with absolute certainty" is about to collapse and kill everyone inside. If the inhabitants ignore our repeated warnings to get out, then what should we do? Should we rescue them against their wills and then reason with them afterwards? Yes, said Augustine: "I think that if we abstained from doing it, we should well deserve the charge of cruelty." But suppose that, as we undertake our forcible rescue, all occupants except one kill themselves by leaping out of high windows? Should we blame ourselves for those deaths? No, said Augustine: "we should console ourselves in our grief for the loss of the rest by the thoughts of the one [who was rescued]; and we should not allow all to perish without a single rescue, in the fear lest the remainder should destroy themselves."

Having laid the altruistic foundation of his argument, Augustine proceeded to its predictable and logical conclusion. If "true reason and benevolence" demand that we forcibly secure the safety of people "for the brief space of their life on earth," then it certainly follows that we should also compel them "in order that men may attain eternal life and escape eternal punishment." Hence, the righteous persecution of heretics is nothing less than a "work of mercy to which we ought to apply ourselves." We should note, however, that Augustine—unlike Thomas Aquinas, John Calvin, and many later defenders of persecution—opposed putting heretics to death. After all, there can be no hope of saving the soul of a dead heretic.

A fascinating feature of Augustine's defense of righteous persecution is its broad application to areas other than religion. The "for their own good" argument is a common justification today for many victimless crime laws in the United States and other countries. The most egregious examples, of course, appear in the rationales for drug laws. Years ago, I discussed this matter in considerable detail in my article "The Righteous Persecution of Drug Consumers." The similarities between the justifications given by modern drug inquisitors and Augustine's arguments for righteous persecution are striking in almost every particular. Here is just one example from my earlier discussion:

> Heretics, Augustine believed, imperil their "spiritual health"; they are destined to suffer the torments of hell. Thus, those who truly "love their neighbor" will recognize their "duty" to compel these "wandering sheep." Righteous persecutors are like physicians who try to help a "raving madman," for heretics "commit murder on their own persons." When motivated by love, persecutors cannot do evil: "Love and you cannot but do well."
>
> In true Augustinian fashion, the modern drug inquisitor seeks to "heal" wayward drug users who "commit murder on their own persons." Indeed, Augustine's defense of righteous persecution anticipates virtually every argument used by drug inquisitors.
>
> For example, our modern inquisitors claim that drug consumers are slaves to evil habits and so require coercive intervention for their own good. Augustine,

too, warned against the "fetters" of sinful habits which have the "strength of iron chains." These evil habits ("a disease of the mind") become a "necessity," forming a "chain" which holds the victim [the heretic] "in the duress of servitude."[1]

The purpose of this detour is to point out that contemporary freethinkers should not be smug about their supposed superiority to early Christians who defended persecution. The particulars may differ, but the essential *form* of Augustine's argument remains in full force among the defenders of drug laws, compulsory medical care, and the many other instances in which a government compels people "for their own good." It took many centuries for Augustine's argument to be decisively refuted, and that required a theory of individual rights of the sort that Libertarians now defend. All freethinkers should keep this lesson in mind.

2

The Problem of Heresy

The problem of heresy (from the Greek *hairesis*, meaning "choice") was a dominant concern of the Catholic Church throughout the later Middle Ages. To understand the reason, we may profitably compare the medieval heretic to his secular analogue: the traitor.

Treason is to the modern state what heresy was to the medieval church. Indeed, the word "traitor" sprang from a religious controversy. *Traditores* ("handers-over") were those Christian bishops who obeyed an edict of the Roman emperor Diocletian (c. 303) to hand over copies of scripture to the state so they could be destroyed. The *traditores* caused a major schism in North Africa, as theologians wrangled over whether *traditores* should be restored to communion and whether bishops who had been *traditores* could perform valid ordinations.

The Donatist schismatics argued that *traditores* had lost all such privileges and that ordinations by such handers-over were invalid. Catholics such as Augustine took the opposite view, maintaining that the spiritual powers of bishops lay in their office and remained valid regardless of the sins of particular bishops. (Augustine believed that the exclusionary policy of the Donatists would prevent the Catholic Church—an organization that included both sinners and saints—from becoming truly universal and would doom it instead to the permanent status of a relatively small group consisting only of the pure.)

Clearly, treason implies betrayal, but one must belong to an organization before one can betray it. That is what distinguishes the "heretic" from the "infidel." The infidel is an outsider, a nonmember who is incapable of betraying a church to which he never belonged. Likewise, a foreigner cannot commit treason against any government but his own.

During the Middle Ages, the individual was inducted into the church through baptism. Since baptism usually occurred during infancy, it could scarcely be called voluntary. Nevertheless, the godparents made promises on behalf of the child that obligated him or her for life. Thereafter, the Christian, bound to the church legally and irrevocably through baptism, was required to defer to official doctrine, as ultimately determined by the pope. In the words of the medieval historian Walter Ullmann, heresy was the sin committed by a Christian who "showed intellectual arrogance by preferring his own opinions to those who were specially qualified to pronounce upon matters of faith."[2] Heresy was more than a sin, however; it was also a crime. The heretic committed high treason against the political authority of the church and endangered the theocratic foundation of government. Orthodoxy (i.e., right thinking) was the ideological bedrock of social and political order, and the heretic threatened to undercut this foundation at its root. The parallels between heresy and treason are therefore more than superficial. Heresy was itself punishable as treason because it subverted the authority of the church from within.

The notion of orthodoxy, per se (i.e., shorn of its religious connotations), is unobjectionable, even to atheists and other freethinkers. An organization must establish an identity by which to distinguish between members and nonmembers. If an organization is ideological in nature, then its identity will be defined by a credo—a set of beliefs or principles that determines the conditions of membership. The ability of that credo to withstand philosophic scrutiny is irrelevant here. Whether rational or irrational, a credo constitutes the "orthodoxy," the intellectual foundation, of an ideological organization.

An organization without an orthodoxy is an organization without ideas.

Thus understood, an orthodox credo is a feature of *all* ideological institutions. Because philosophy normally lacks institutional affiliations, it (ideally) does not have credos, orthodoxies, and heretics. This is the nature of the beast called philosophy, but it does not render philosophers inherently more noble, honest, or undogmatic than their theological cousins. Potential problems for theologians arise because most are at once church members *and* philosophers, and those roles may conflict. If a philosopher joins an ideological organization and commits to its credo, then he too may experience the tension between orthodoxy and heresy—between loyalty to an organization (or movement) and loyalty to the voice of reason. I see no evidence to suggest that philosophers, if confronted with this decision, will necessarily choose better than theologians.

When viewed in an institutional setting, the ideas of orthodoxy and heresy, broadly conceived, are neither irrational nor dangerous—so long, that is, as membership in an institution is *voluntary*. Dissenters are free to quit an organization or never to join at all. That was the case with early Christianity before it became the state religion in fourth-century Rome. Christianity was more than a theology; it was also an organization, and as such it needed to forge an orthodoxy, an intellectual identity, a set of beliefs that unified its members. A heretic in those circumstances might be expelled or banned from a particular organization, but he would remain free to go his own way.

Only after Christians acquired the reins of state power and substituted *force* for *persuasion* did their notions of orthodoxy and heresy become dangerous. Through the instrumentality of government, what had been orthodoxy for a single religious movement became orthodoxy for *society as a whole*. As the distinguished medievalist R. W. Southern observed, "the church was a compulsory society in precisely the same way as the modern state is a compulsory society."[3] As the good of the church became synonymous with the good of society, heretics became more than wayward members of an organization— they became threats to the foundations of social order. This transformation was caused not by the notion of orthodoxy, per se, but by the *politicizing* of orthodoxy.

Heretics were ferociously persecuted by Catholic authorities at various times during the Middle Ages. One of the most atrocious examples occurred in the early 13th century in southern France, during what is usually called the Albigensian crusade. Thousands of heretical "Cathars" were slaughtered indiscriminately—men, women, and children alike—and entire towns were devastated, even though the Cathars kept to themselves and threatened nobody. Upon learning of those wholesale massacres, a delighted Pope Innocent III gave thanks for a double blessing: wicked heretics were being killed, and their killers were that much closer to attaining salvation. As that supposedly great pope put it,

> God hath mercifully purged His people's land and the pest of heretical wickedness . . . is being deadened and driven away. . . . Wherefore we give praise and thanks to God almighty, because in one and the same cause of His mercy, He hath deigned to work two works of justice, by bringing upon these faithless folks their merited destruction, in such a fashion that as many as possible of the faithful should gain their well-earned reward by the "extermination" of those folk.[4]

Historians have long been aware that medieval religious persecution—which became centralized under papal control (known as the Holy Office of the Inquisition) not long after the Albigensian crusade—often had political undercurrents. But some of those historians have offered a defense (of sorts) of the persecutors. We are told that rulers and church authorities were generally more lenient and open-minded than the people they ruled. As R. W. Southern put it, "on the whole the holders of ecclesiastic authority were less prone to violence, even against unbelievers, than the people whom they ruled."[5] According to another historian, heretics "aroused intense feelings of fear and hatred among the mass of the people because they dissociated themselves completely from all the values on which society was based." [6]

That conventional interpretation was challenged by R. I. Moore in a brilliant and provocative book, *The Formation of a Persecuting Society: Power and Deviance in Western Europe* (1987; 2nd ed., 2007). Moore questioned whether the masses feared and despised heretics as much as some historians have claimed; on the contrary, heresies often attracted substantial segments of the population. Generally speaking, according to Moore, it is not true that "medieval man" feared and resented any deviation from the Catholic faith; rather, "the reason why preachers of heresy were denounced, pursued and extinguished by whatever means availed was precisely the fear that they would undermine the faith of the *simplices*, and with it the social order." After examining various cases in which heretics appear to have been executed by public demand, Moore concluded that "on inspection their numbers shrink rapidly."

According to Moore, we possess "no true evidence of general popular antipathy to heresy as such." Thus, medieval persecutors were not "agents of society at large, at least if our conception of society is one which includes the great majority of its members." Persecutors had their own agenda; heretics were a political threat because they declared "their own independence of the structures of established power. They looked for their authority to those who heard them." Emerging bureaucratic regimes stigmatized and persecuted heretics—along with Jews, homosexuals, witches, and even lepers—as a means to consolidate and justify their own power.

3

Aquinas, Luther, and Calvin on Persecution

As the Catholic Church went about exterminating heretics in the 13th century, major intellectuals rallied to her defense. Thomas Aquinas (1225–1274)—a Dominican whose order had been specifically charged by the pope with rooting out heresy—discussed heresy in detail in his voluminous *Summa Theologica*, and his views profoundly influenced church policy. (In 1542, when Pope Paul III reconstituted the Holy Office of the Inquisition in Rome, he relied heavily on the arguments of Aquinas.)

Aquinas, like Catholic theologians before him, distinguished between unbelief and heresy. Pure unbelievers are those who have never accepted the Christian religion, such as Jews and Muslims. Those unbelievers should be punished if they blaspheme or commit other sins, but they should not be forced to embrace Christianity. But heretics are a different matter, because heresy is a special kind of unbelief "pertaining to those who profess the Christian faith, but corrupt its dogmas."

Unlike pure unbelievers, heretics should be compelled to accept the correct doctrines. Heresy involves more than error; it is *obstinate* error. Simple error may be innocent, but if the heretic persists in his error after being corrected by church authorities, then his error becomes willful—the result of egoistic pride. When that happens, the heretic should be punished. Why? Because heretics, having pledged themselves to God via the Catholic Church, "should be submitted even to bodily compulsion, that they may fulfill what they have promised, and hold what they at one time received."

The heretic betrays his pledge to God and thereby corrupts the very religion he professes to accept. This affront to God, explained Aquinas, deserves the death penalty:

> Heretics deserve not only to be separated from the Church by excommunication, but also to be severed from the world by death. For it is a much graver matter to corrupt the faith which quickens the soul,

20

than to forge money, which supports temporal life. Therefore, if forgers of money and other evil-doers are condemned to death at once by the secular authority, much more reason is there for heretics, as soon as they are convicted of heresy, to be not only excommunicated, but even put to death.

Although heretics deserve death for the first offense, the church, merciful as always, should not inflict this penalty until the second relapse into heresy. Thus, the reasoned barbarism of Aquinas surpassed even that of Augustine, who had favored mere fines and banishment as penalties for heresy.

The Catholic Church regarded 16th-century Protestants as heretics worthy of death, and many of them paid that price. It is hardly surprising, therefore, that leading Protestant Reformers defended some measure of toleration, at least for themselves. Most of those same leaders, however, also defended the persecution of Catholics and even heretics among their fellow Protestants. When accused of inconsistency, those Janus-faced Protestants typically replied in the same manner as did John Calvin. Namely, the right to persecute error does not entail the right to persecute truth. Protestant leaders were absolutely certain that their doctrines, and their doctrines alone, were correct; thus, they had the right to preach the truth, as well as the right to suppress religious error by violent means, if necessary.

In 1523, shortly after Martin Luther split from the Catholic Church (and while his life was still in danger), he published a passionate defense of toleration. Luther cited "the well-known saying, found also in Augustine, 'No one can or ought to be constrained to believe.'" He then summarized this time-honored argument: "it is useless and impossible to command or compel any one by force to believe one thing or another. It must be taken hold of in a different way; force cannot accomplish it." Luther thus proclaimed the inability of persecution to accomplish its intended goal: "Heresy can never be prevented by force." If God's word (the Bible) and persuasion do not correct heretics, then "the end . . . will remain unaccomplished through secular power, though it fill the world with blood."[7]

Luther conceded that persecution can compel "by word and deed." But such outward conformity, when it does not flow from inner conviction, is sheer hypocrisy devoid of religious significance. Persecutors "cannot constrain [the heart], though they wear themselves out trying. For the proverb is true, Thoughts are free." Salvation is an unmerited gift freely bestowed by God "to which no one can be forced. Nay, it is a divine work, done in the Spirit, certainly not a matter which outward authority should compel or create."

If Luther had written nothing else on toleration, he might have received accolades from future generations, believers and unbelievers alike. But as sympathetic biographers might say, Luther was a complex man, an unsystematic thinker who advocated different policies at different times. Or as unsympathetic biographers might say, an older Luther—ensconced in power, his life and future secure—betrayed his principles and turned from persecuted to persecutor.

Whatever the correct explanation may be, there is no doubt that Luther, after aligning himself with sympathetic German princes (many of whom were more interested in power and looting Catholic property than in religious doctrine), became a fierce advocate of persecution. We see this in Luther's attitude toward the Anabaptists, or "rebaptizers" (a misleading label foisted upon them by their enemies)—those Protestants who believed in adult baptism and mocked infant baptism as "the popish bath." Anabaptists were savagely persecuted by both Catholics and Protestants, and many thousands were cruelly tortured and slain. Protestants were especially fond of "baptizing" Anabaptist heretics by drowning them in rivers.

Luther initially defended freedom for Anabaptists (except the small minority who resorted to violence). Later, though, he called for the extermination of all heretics, along with

Catholics who did not acknowledge themselves enemies of Christ and the emperor:

> Heretics are not to be disputed with, but to be condemned unheard, and whilst they perish by fire, the faithful ought to pursue the evil to its source, and bathe their hands in the blood of the Catholic bishops, and of the Pope, who is a devil in disguise.[8]

Jews also felt the sting of the hateful intolerance of the older Luther:

> Burn the synagogues; take away their books, including the Bible. They should be compelled to work, denied food and shelter, preferably banished. If they mention the name of God, report them to the magistrate or throw Saudreck [pig dung] on them. Moses said that idolaters should not be tolerated. If he were here he would be the first to burn their synagogues.[9]

Even in later life, Luther sometimes defended what he called "freedom of conscience" (a phrase he may have coined). However, he meant only the freedom to believe as one likes, according to one's own judgment. Those beliefs could include heretical beliefs, provided one kept them to oneself. Once the heretic talked about his beliefs, or attempted to communicate them to others in any manner, or engaged in heretical rituals, then he should be subject to the force of Christian law. In short, for the older Luther "freedom of conscience" signified the right to believe as you like, so long as you remain silent about any heretical beliefs you may have. Freedom of conscience did not include freedom of speech or worship, for those practices might easily infect others and lead them into heresy as well.

If Martin Luther provided erratic support for toleration, another great Reformer, the Frenchman John Calvin, provided none at all. As an eminent Christian biographer of Calvin once quipped, if someone claims to find a single word in favor of toleration in Calvin's voluminous writings, it must be a misprint. Although Calvin rejected Catholicism, he embraced the Catholic policy of persecution: "Because the Papists persecute the truth, should we on that account refrain from repressing error?"

As a believer in predestination, Calvin understood that persecution cannot save souls: the elect were selected by God before creation. But Calvin insisted that heresy and blasphemy (the two concepts were sometimes used interchangeably by Protestant champions of persecution) insult the supreme majesty of God and should be punished for that reason. The punishment of heretics and blasphemers vindicates the honor of God.

Calvin was the hardest among hard-liners. Under no circumstances should secular authorities tolerate heretics and blasphemers. Indeed, "those who would spare heretics and blasphemers are themselves blasphemers." The "implacable severity" of the death penalty is mandatory because "devotion to God's honor should be preferred to all human concerns." In pursuit of that end, we "should expunge from memory our mutual humanity" as we exterminate heretics and blasphemers with righteous zeal.

Calvin proved as good as his word. In 1553, he engineered the gruesome execution of the Spaniard Michael Servetus, a brilliant philosopher, scientist, and physician who is credited with discovering the pulmonary circulation of blood. Servetus was adjudged a criminal for two primary reasons, each punishable by death in Roman law. He rejected the Trinity as a needless, incomprehensible doctrine, and he denied the efficacy of infant baptism. (Having repudiated the canon law of the Catholic Church, Protestants typically appealed instead to the ancient Code of Justinian for legal justification of their judicial murders.)

While hiding in France under an assumed name, Servetus sent a manuscript copy of his last book, *The Restoration of Christianity*, to Calvin in Geneva. Servetus apparently hoped the great Reformer would view the book sympathetically—a naïve and fatal miscalculation. Calvin never returned the manuscript; he had a better use for it. He gave four incriminating pages to a colleague, Guillaume Trie, who forwarded them to a Catholic correspondent in France. Trie also revealed the true identity of "Villanovanus," the pseudonym used by Servetus. The Protestant Trie chided French Catholics for tolerating this heretic in their midst:

> You suffer a heretic, who well deserves to be burned wherever he may be. I have in mind a man who will be condemned by the Papists as much by us or ought to be. . . . Where I'd like to know is the zeal which you pretend? Where is the police of this fine hierarchy of which you so boast?

The tactic of Calvin and Trie almost worked. Servetus was arrested and convicted of heresy by Catholic authorities; but before he could be roasted over a Catholic fire, he managed to escape from prison and head for Italy. Unfortunately, for reasons known only to himself, Servetus chose a route that took him through Calvin's Geneva. There, he was quickly recognized and, in an indictment drawn up by Calvin, charged with 39 counts of heresy and blasphemy. Servetus was sentenced to death for attempting "to infect the world with [his] stinking heretical poison."[10]

On October 27, 1553, Servetus was bound to a stake with a rope twisted around his neck, his book tied to an arm, and a Protestant fire—fueled by green wood to make it burn slowly—stirring below. It took 30 minutes for Servetus to die, but by all accounts he suffered the ordeal bravely. Defenders of Calvin like to point out that he favored the more merciful execution of beheading rather than burning but was overruled by Genevan officials. If that qualifies as a point in Calvin's favor, so be it. In my judgment, among major thinkers the western world has rarely if ever seen a more intolerant, arrogant, and sadistic mentality than the mind of John Calvin.

4

Shaftesbury on the Value of Ridicule

In English prosecutions for blasphemy, which extended well into the 19th century, prosecutors typically applauded England for its freedom of speech and press. But this freedom, they went on to say, had its limits; it did not include the right to treat the Christian religion with contempt and ridicule. Criticisms of Christianity were legal, but only if done in a serious, respectful manner. Ridicule, however, was a common tactic of freethinkers, so their convictions were virtually guaranteed. For example, George W. Foote, liberal editor of the *Freethinker*, delighted in publishing satirical essays and cartoons that lampooned Christianity, and these efforts earned him a year in prison in 1883. (The salesman and printer of the *Freethinker* were also prosecuted. For Foote's account of his trial, see his *Prisoner for Blasphemy*, 1886.)

Foote's *Comic Bible Sketches*, which were published regularly in the *Freethinker*, played a major role in his prosecution. Foote was straightforward about his reason for publishing the sketches, which were quickly reprinted by French freethinkers:

> We honestly admit that our purpose is to discredit the Bible as the infallible word of God. Believing as we do, with Voltaire, that despotism can never be abolished without destroying the dogmas on which it rests, and that the Bible is the grand source and sanction of them all, we are profoundly anxious to expose its pretension.

Foote's offensive cartoons and the controversy they provoked bring to mind the recent massacre of the 12 cartoonists and staff members of the French satirical magazine *Charlie Hebdo*. Both cases provoked debates about whether freedom of speech and press may be carried too far, as when satirists deliberately offend Muslims by making fun of their sincere religious beliefs. As with most other controversies, however, this one is nothing new—except that in earlier centuries, it was Christians who argued that their religion should be exempt from public ridicule and that offenders should be silenced by legal means.

Early freethinkers constituted the shock troops in the campaign to remove all legal liability for freedom of speech and press, including the ridicule of Christianity and other religions, however offensive their buffoonery may be. Some freethinkers paid a heavy personal price in this campaign. In the early 19th century, for example, the English freethought publisher Richard Carlile served more than nine years in prison; and his wife, sister, and many dozens of his workers were imprisoned as well—for an early display of mass civil disobedience. (See chapter 7 for the details of the Carlile prosecutions.)

The foremost defender of ridicule in every area, especially religion, was the freethinker and deist Anthony Ashley Cooper (1671–1713), better known as Lord Shaftesbury. In the first two parts of *Characteristics of Men, Manners, Opinions, and Times*—a collection of previously published essays first published in 1711 and subsequently expanded—Shaftesbury, a classical liberal, presented a fascinating defense of the personal and social benefits of ridicule and satire, and his remarks profoundly influenced later freethinkers. I discuss Shaftesbury and his influence in this chapter and the next.

Shaftesbury repudiated the notion that some doctrines are so important or sacred as to render them exempt from any and all ridicule. Any such claim is bound to foster pretentiousness:

> There can be no impartial and free censure of manners where any peculiar custom or national opinion is set apart, and not only exempted from criticism but even flattered with the highest art. It is only in a free nation, such as ours, that imposture has no privilege and that neither the credit of a court, the power of a nobility, nor the awfulness of a church can give her protection or hinder her from being arraigned in every shape and appearance.

But what if ridicule is pushed too far? Is it wrong to ridicule beliefs that many people hold as sacred? Shaftesbury pointed out that we are apt to become offended when our *own* beliefs are ridiculed, even though we may not hesitate to ridicule the beliefs of others. "But who shall be judge of what may be freely examined and what may not, where liberty may be used and where it may not? What remedy shall we prescribe to this in general?" Freedom itself, according to Shaftesbury, is its own remedy. Trial and experience will eventually reveal when ridicule is appropriate and when it is not. Many religious believers will claim that their beliefs are so sacred and beyond reproach that anyone who ridicules them should be punished. "'Oh,' say we, 'the subjects are too grave.'"

> Perhaps so, but let us see first whether they are really grave or no, for, in the manner we may conceive them they may peradventure be very grave and weighty in our imagination, but very ridiculous and impertinent in their own nature. Gravity is of the very essence of imposture. . . . Now what rule or measure is there in the world except in the considering of the real temper of things, to find which are truly serious and which ridiculous? And how can this be done unless by applying the ridicule to see whether it will bear? . . .
>
> *Mirth, for the most part, cuts through weighty matters with greater firmness and ease than seriousness.*

Like other classical liberals of his time, Shaftesbury compared freedom of discussion to free trade. Just as free trade will bring about an equilibrium between supply and demand, free discussion will eventually discredit (at least among serious thinkers) "scurrilous buffoonery" that is inappropriately crude: "By freedom of conversation, this illiberal kind of wit will lose its credit."

> For wit is its own remedy. Liberty and commerce bring it to its true standard. The only danger is the

laying an embargo. The same thing happens here as in the case of trade. Impositions and restrictions reduce it to a low ebb. Nothing is so advantageous to it as a free port.

Freedom of discussion is the foundation of civil discourse:

All politeness is owing to liberty. We polish one another and rub off our corners and rough sides by a sort of amicable collision. To restrain this is inevitably to bring a rust upon men's understandings. It is a destroying of civility, good breeding and even charity itself, under pretence of maintaining it.

Shaftesbury called attention to the hypocrisy of many religious zealots who engaged in debates with "our modern free-writers" (i.e., deists and other critics of Christianity). While appearing to engage in open discussions with religious skeptics, these "Janus-faced" champions of Christianity were quick to call on government to enforce blasphemy laws and other oppressive measures to silence their adversaries: "Having entered the lists and agreed to the fair laws of combat by wit and argument, they have no sooner proved their weapon than you hear them crying aloud for help and delivering over to the secular arm." Shaftesbury's mention of the "secular arm" was probably a tacit reference to Catholicism. Since the Catholic Church was technically forbidden to shed blood, it turned heretics and blasphemers over to the "secular arm" for punishment, with the clear understanding that they would be put to death. John Milton and other liberal Protestants had condemned persecution as a uniquely Catholic policy, one that Protestants should not emulate. Thus, in referring specifically to the "secular arm," Shaftesbury was following suit. To link a policy directly to Catholicism was to discredit that policy among many Protestants.

Shaftesbury had many other interesting things to say about the benefits of free and open public discussions. Consider his reply to the objection that unrestrained debates about religion will often generate an uncertainty that may lead to disbelief or skepticism. Reasoning is mental labor, and, as with other kinds of labor, people will not engage in serious reasoning unless they find it agreeable in some way. The unrestrained freedom to use wit and raillery provides this kind of incentive:

> It is the habit of reasoning alone which can make a reasoner. And men can never be better invited to the habit than when they find pleasure in it. A freedom of raillery, a liberty in decent language to question everything, and an allowance of unravelling or

refuting any argument without offence to the arguer, are the only terms which can render such speculative conversations any way agreeable. For to say truth, they have been rendered burdensome to mankind by the strictness of the laws prescribed to them and by the prevailing pedantry and bigotry of those who reign in them and assume to themselves to be dictators in these provinces.

Shaftesbury's defense of wit and ridicule bore fruit among freethinkers. Although Voltaire is the best-known example of a freethinker who used ridicule and humor in his criticism of Christianity, he was far from the only freethinker who used this tactic. Consider the case of Thomas Woolston (1669–1733), a Cambridge graduate admired by Voltaire, who was the most vilified of the deistic critics of orthodox Christianity. Woolston's sarcastic criticisms of a literal belief in the Bible brought accusations of insanity—"poor mad Woolston, most scandalous of the deists," as the 19th-century historian Leslie Stephen put it in *History of English Thought in the Eighteenth Century* (1876). According to Stephen (who was himself an agnostic), Woolston attacked the Gospel narratives as "preposterous," and this "would have been sufficient of itself to raise doubts of its author's sanity." Stephen considered

Woolston "a mere buffoon jingling his cap and bells in a sacred shrine." Even Stephen admitted, however, that there are "queer gleams of distorted sense, and even of literary power, in the midst of his buffoonery." (A good deal of abusive sarcasm may be found in the writings of 18th-century critics of deism, but none of those respectable Christian writers, so far as I know, was ever accused of being insane.)

Woolston believed that "hireling preachers" were conspiring against him—another indication of his paranoid insanity, according to Stephen. Yet Woolston's fear of persecution proved well founded. In 1729, he was convicted of blasphemy, fined 100 pounds, and sentenced to a year in prison. Then, unable to pay a security of 2,000 pounds to insure his future good conduct, Woolston is reported to have spent the remaining three years of his life in prison. (Voltaire, who was in England at the time, disputed the claim that Woolston died in prison. "Several of my friends have seen him in his house; he died there, at liberty." The great historian of freethought, J. M. Robertson, attempted to reconcile these conflicting accounts by suggesting that Woolston may have been under some kind of house arrest during his last three years.)

A contemporary critic charged Woolston with "scurrilous buffoonery and gross raillery," a charge that has been echoed by modern historians. For example, in *Reason and Authority in the Eighteenth Century* (1964), G. R. Cragg called Woolston's criticism of the Bible "hysterically abusive." But few if any historians mention the reason for Woolston's "abusive" tactics. In a passage that reads like a less sophisticated version of Shaftesbury's arguments in favor of ridicule, Woolston wrote the following:

> I am resolved to give the Letter of the Scripture no Rest, so long as God gives me Life and Abilities to attack it. . . . And how then is such a Work to be performed to best Advantage? Is it to be done in a grave, sedate, and serious Manner? No, I think Ridicule should here take the Place of sober Reasoning, as the more proper and effectual means to cure Men of their foolish Faith and absurd Notions. As no wise Man hardly ever reprehends a Blunderbuss for his Bull, any other way, than by laughing at him; so the Asserters of nonsensical Notions in Theology should, if possible, be satirized and jested upon, or they will never . . . desert their absurd Doctrines.

5

How Freethinkers Attempted to Avoid Persecution

In the previous chapter, I discussed Shaftesbury's defense of ridicule in matters of religion. We all have basic beliefs, whether in religion or in other areas, that we regard as so important—or "sacred" in the broad sense—that we may become deeply offended when others use wit and sarcasm to indicate that they do not take our beliefs seriously. But we cannot expect our personal beliefs to be taken seriously by others unless we are willing to defend those beliefs with rational arguments.

To become so apoplectic when our beliefs are ridiculed that we demand the punishment of our critics is to exhibit an unwillingness to engage in rational discourse. Truly reasonable beliefs will withstand ridicule and thereby command widespread respect, whereas irrational beliefs will be unable to withstand ridicule and thereby lose credibility in the public eye. Thus, according to Shaftesbury, ridicule is not an unfortunate byproduct of freedom of speech and press; on the contrary, ridicule serves a *positive* social function by helping us to distinguish beliefs that should be taken seriously from those that should not. Over time, as some beliefs prove their mettle and become widely accepted, they will become less subject to ridicule.

Shaftesbury made additional observations about the effects of legal restraints on the freedom of speech and press. In an age of blasphemy laws and other types of censorship, when religious and political dissenters were not free to say what they really thought, those dissenters often resorted to various literary devices to avoid punishment. Shaftesbury put it this way:

> If men are forbid to speak their minds seriously on certain subjects, they will do it ironically. If they are forbid to speak at all upon such subjects or if they find it really dangerous to do so, they will then redouble their disguise, involve themselves in mysteriousness

and talk so as hardly to be understood, or at least not plainly interpreted, by those who are disposed to do them mischief.

Long before Shaftesbury wrote that passage, freethinkers had attempted to avoid legal penalties by using literary devices that might conceal their true opinions. One such tactic was to write dialogues with two or more fictional characters. A dialogue permitted the villain of the piece to express unorthodox beliefs, which the orthodox character (the ostensible stand-in for the writer) would then refute. But when freethinkers used this tactic, their unorthodox arguments were typically stronger than their orthodox refutations, which made some readers suspicious.

A famous example of this tactic—one with tragic consequences—occurred with an Italian freethinker named Giulio Cesare Vanini (1585–1619). Vanini traveled extensively throughout Europe and wrote a number of Latin treatises that expressed highly unorthodox religious beliefs, but he always provided supposed refutations of those scandalous doctrines. In one book, for example, he explained in considerable detail the "problem of evil"—an argument against the traditional concept of God that was first expressed by some ancient Greek skeptics. Vanini then replied to that important argument, but his counterarguments lacked the clarity and logical force of the initial presentation.

The same problem appeared in Vanini's discussions of personal immortality. Vanini admired both Aristotle and the Renaissance Aristotelian Pietro Pomponazzi, and he incorporated some of their arguments against personal immortality into his works. Of course, Vanini proceeded to refute those naturalistic arguments and to defend the immortality of the soul; but, again, his refutations left much to be desired. Nevertheless, the tactic permitted Vanini to pose as a champion of Christian orthodoxy.

The ruse caught up with Vanini in his last book, the final section of which includes a dialogue between two major characters: "Julius Caesar" (who was supposed to represent Vanini's own beliefs) and "Alexander." At various points, Vanini injected heretical and skeptical views into the conversation, preceding them with qualifications such as "If I were not a Christian," or "If I were not instructed by the Church," or "If I were not a believer," I would say. . . . The deception became even more obvious when a third character, the "Atheist of Amsterdam," entered the conversation. The atheist made outrageous comments—for example, claiming that the Christian martyrs were probably mentally ill—only to be met with weak retorts.

One exchange in particular clearly illustrates Vanini's tactic. Here is a passage that he attributed to the Atheist of Amsterdam:

> According to the Bible, one would assume that the Devil was stronger than God. Against the will of God, Adam and Eve sinned and thus perished the human race. The Son of God, coming to remedy this fault, was condemned by his judges, incited by the Devil, to an ignominious death. So, according to the Bible, the satanic will is stronger than God's. Lo! God wants all men to be saved; but he saves only very few. On the contrary, the Devil wishes all men damned and their number is infinite. Out of the vast world, only those people who live in Italy, Spain, some districts of France, Germany, and Poland have any chance for salvation. If one deducts from these candidates for redemption Jews, secret heretics, atheists, blasphemers, simonists, adulterers, and sodomites who are not likely to inherit the Kingdom of Heaven, scarcely a squad remains compared to the millions who will be damned.

As that passage illustrates, Vanini often injected wit into his presentation of heretical opinions; but, witty or no, it was unthinkable that the blasphemies of the atheist should be allowed to stand without a crushing rebuttal. So how did "Julius Caesar" respond to the Atheist of Amsterdam? Well, Julius conceded that Satan won the first round with God (in the Garden of Eden), but noted that God won the second round (with the mission of Jesus). Julius also pointed out that the huge number of people in hell would generate an enormous amount of labor, trouble, and aggravation for the demons who managed that place of torment. After hearing several other feeble refutations, the Atheist of Amsterdam praised Julius for his powerful arguments, calling him "the world's leading antagonist of atheism."

It scarcely took a genius to understand what Vanini was up to in his dialogues, but his book initially passed inspection by papal censors, who declared that it contained nothing contrary or repugnant to the Catholic faith. Whether those censors were afflicted by bureaucratic laziness or stupidity, or both, is impossible to say, but more intelligent Catholic persecutors eventually caught on to Vanini's game. On February 9, 1619, the Holy Office of the Inquisition in Rome convicted Vanini of "atheism, blasphemies, impieties, and other crimes" and sentenced him to be executed the same day. The sentence read as follows:

> [Vanini shall] be delivered into the hands of the executioner of justice, who shall draw him upon a hurdle,

in his shirt, with a halter about his neck, and bearing upon his shoulders a placard with the words ATHE-IST AND BLASPHEMER OF THE NAME OF GOD; he shall thus conduct him before the principal entrance to the metropolitan church of St. Stephen, and being there placed on his knees with head and feet naked, holding in his hands a lighted wax-torch, he shall ask pardon from God, from the King, and from Justice for his said blasphemies; afterwards he shall bring him into the Place of Salin, and, bound to a stake there erected, he shall cut off his tongue, and strangle him, and afterwards his body shall be burnt at the stake-fire, there prepared, and the ashes thrown to the wind.

As Vanini was taken from prison to be placed on the hurdle, he cried out, "Let us go, let us go joyfully to die, as becomes a philosopher!" Vanini spurned the crucifix offered to him and refused to confess any guilt. Then, after being bound to the stake, he refused to extend his tongue so it could be cut off, so the executioner wrenched his mouth open, pulled out his tongue with iron pincers, and then used a knife to finish the job. At this point, with blood flowing, Vanini screamed in pain—a sound that one pious observer gleefully compared to the bellowing of an ox that was being slaughtered. Strangulation and burning quickly followed.

Another literary tactic popular among freethinkers was to criticize pagan beliefs and practices that resembled those of Christianity, while disingenuously claiming that such criticisms did not apply to Christianity. Many deists used this tactic to avoid punishment, but I will confine this discussion to how it was employed by Charles Blount (1654–1693), one of the most radical and influential anti-Christian deists of his era.

Consider *Great Is Diana of the Ephesians* (1680), Blount's thinly veiled attack on Christian rituals, dogmas, and clergy. Blount's stated purpose was to criticize ancient heathen religions, which, under the auspices of self-serving and ignorant priests, had become encrusted with absurd dogmas and rituals. Blount, proposing to examine those heathen religions critically, wrote the following:

> Now most religions (excepting ours), being tainted with the Interest of the Clergy, [we] must examine and consider them accordingly: For if a Porter should come and tell me, he had brought me such a Letter from my Father, and the first part of the Letter should teach Obedience to Parents, but the latter part of it

should command me to give the said Porter half my
Estate; in this case I should (notwithstanding the
Testimony of his Brother Porters), without some further demonstration, believe the Letter a Counterfeit;
as also that the first part of it, which taught Obedience, was only to make way for the second and principal clause, the giving the Porter Money. Now most
of the Heathen Priests were such Porters. . . .

To debunk the "mysteries" of heathen religions may have
seemed unnecessary when addressing Christian readers.
Blount's subtext was clear to any reader who was half-awake,
despite disclaimers such as "what I have here written concerns
[Heathenish Religions] only." Again, while commenting on
heathen sacrifices, Blount noted that his criticisms might
seem to apply to Moses as well, but he reassured his audience
in a not-very-convincing fashion:

Now if any Hypocrite to glorifie his own zeal, should
pretend that a discourse of this nature does through
the Heathen Sacrifices, reproach those of Moses,
which resembled them in outward appearance, he
must retrieve himself from that error, if he rightly
apprehends the difference.

Just what *was* the difference between heathen sacrifices and those commanded by Moses? It was this: Heathen priests concocted sacrifices as a means to hoodwink and bilk their followers, whereas Moses was directed by the "true God." That is all Blount said on the matter, so little wonder that pious readers rightly suspected him of duplicity. Christianity, not heathenism, was Blount's real target—but that target, protected by law, could not be aimed at safely, without fear of punishment.

6

The English Deists

In previous chapters, I had occasion to mention deism and some particular deists, such as Shaftesbury and Charles Blount. It is now time that I explain this movement—and it is, I think, proper to call deism a "movement"—and its doctrines.

During its heyday in the 18th century, deism was closely affiliated with classical liberalism. More than a few deists, such as John Toland, were active in the radical wing of liberalism, sometimes called "radical (or real) whiggism," or (in the case of those liberals who rejected monarchy altogether) "radical republicanism." For example, two writers familiar to many libertarians—John Trenchard and Thomas Gordon, authors of the libertarian classic *Cato's Letters*—wrote many anti-clerical tracts, most of which appeared in their journal, the *Independent Whig*. Though, like most deists of their time, Trenchard and Gordon never expressly repudiated Christianity, they did call for a return to "primitive Christianity"— that is, a return to the moral teachings of Jesus, which every deist praised. (Paul was the favorite New Testament target of deists, primarily because he developed the doctrine of original sin.) According to this typical deistic agenda, we should reject the irrational doctrines and practices that had been added to primitive Christianity by self-serving priests and theologians; instead, we should embrace the pure, undefiled *moral* teachings of Jesus. According to the deists, the essence of Christianity is moral behavior, not belief in dogmas about "mysteries," such as the Trinity, which no one can understand or rationally justify.

In 1754, the English Presbyterian minister John Leland published *A View of the Principal Deistical Writers*, a book that he later expanded into two volumes. In this work, which became the standard secondary source on deism for many years, Leland traced the label "deist" to 1563, when it was used in a book by the Swiss Calvinist Peter Viret. Leland got his information from the massive and highly influential *Historical and Critical Dictionary*, by the infamous skeptic Pierre Bayle (1647–1706). Bayle's *Dictionary* (which today would be called an encyclopedia) provided a gold mine of information for Enlightenment freethinkers, including information about some very obscure figures. In the article on "Viret," Bayle quoted a lengthy passage written by Viret in which he lamented the rise of a new species of unbelievers in France who called themselves "deists." The passage reads, in part,

> I hear that some of this band call themselves Deists, a new word in opposition to that of Atheists. For the word Atheist signifies one that is without God, so they would hereby signify, that they are not without God, because they believe that there is one, whom they even acknowledge for creator of Heaven and Earth, as well as the Turks: but as for Jesus Christ, they do not know who he is, nor do they believe in him or his doctrine. These Deists of whom we speak ridicule all religion, though they accommodate themselves to the religion with whom they are obliged to live, out of complaisance or fear: some among them have a kind of notion of the immortality of the soul; others agree with the Epicureans on that as well as on the Divine providence with regard to mankind: they think he doth not intermeddle with human affairs, and that they are governed by fortune, or by the prudence and folly of men, according as things happen.[11]

Viret was distressed because some of the self-styled deists also called themselves Christians, despite their total rejection of supernatural revelation. (This practice persisted throughout the history of deism, thereby generating the problem of who was really a Christian and who was not.) Viret was also puzzled because many of the deists were highly educated:

> I am struck with horror, when I think that there are such monsters among those who bear the name of Christians. But my horror is redoubled, when I consider that several of those who make profession of learning and human Philosophy, and even are frequently esteemed the most learned, most acute and most subtle genius's, are not only infected with this execrable Atheism, but also profess to teach it, and poison several persons with this venom.[12]

Viret had ridiculed the beliefs of Catholics and Muslims, but he sensed that the deists would not be so easy to dispose of, especially since they explicitly repudiated atheism—a position that virtually no one in the 16th century would embrace. The ongoing conflict between Protestants and Catholics gave Europeans two religions from which to choose, and Viret had no doubt that Protestantism had the upper hand from a biblical perspective. (Islam, which Viret condemned as a type of idolatry, was not a realistic candidate.) But the deists had muddied the waters by offering the third option of no religion at all, in effect, despite their belief in a God of nature:

> Wherefore we live in a time when we are in danger of having more difficulty in contending with these monsters, than with the superstitious and idolators, if God doth not, which I hope he will, prevent it. For amongst the present difference in religion, several very much abuse the liberty given them of choosing which of the two contending religions they will adhere to. For several are of neither, and indeed live without any religion. And if those who have no good opinion of any religion, would content themselves to perish alone in their error and Atheism, without infecting or corrupting others by their wicked discourses and example, and leading them into the same perdition with themselves, this evil would not be so deplorable as it is.[13]

Deism became popular in England around the same time as in France and Holland. In one of the best histories of deism ever written, *The Dynamics of Religion*, the freethought historian J. M. Robertson attributed the rise of deism to a widespread disillusionment with the practical effects of Christianity. Many people had become sick of the incessant internecine conflicts among Christians themselves—the intolerance, cruel persecutions of heretics, witch hunts, and bloody wars that had plagued Europe since the Reformation. Robertson wrote the following:

> Of such general distaste for Christian dogma in the France of 1650, and in the England of 1660–1730, there seems to be only one explanation—namely, that the very extremity of religious feeling, the long frenzy of mutual malevolence, the stupendous failure of a professedly love-inculcating religion to make men so much as consent to let each other alone, much less to love one another, had sent many men on questioning whether the game was worth the candle; whether this creed, which caused blood to flow like water, was any more divine in its special dogmas than that of Mohamet, or those of pagan antiquity. Educated men simply grew sick of the religious temper, of religious phraseology, of religious books, of religious principles; and even those who remained orthodox tended to take on a new tone of secular ratiocination.[14]

Although deism emerged simultaneously in several countries, English deism was destined to exert the most influence. Many French freethinkers veered in the direction of outright atheism, especially during the 18th-century Enlightenment. The majority of 18th-century English freethinkers, though, took the less disturbing route of defending the existence of a benevolent God who created the universe but who thereafter adopted a laissez-faire policy, leaving the universe alone to operate according to natural laws. It was this English tradition that influenced leading American deists such as Thomas Jefferson, James Madison, and Benjamin Franklin; and when Thomas Paine published his notorious defense of deism, *The Age of Reason* (published in two parts, in 1794 and 1795, with a third part—a criticism of biblical prophecies—added in 1807), he drew heavily from his English predecessors, such as Anthony Collins.

Edward Herbert (Lord Cherbury) has traditionally been called the "father" of English deism. In 1624, while serving as England's ambassador to France, Herbert published *De Veritate* (*On Truth*). The book lamented the disunion and disarray of Christianity, which had splintered into a "multitude of sects, divisions, sub-divisions, and cross-divisions." Herbert proposed a solution: five "common notions" which, he argued, are found in all great religions and which would therefore unite them in a common cause. Without these common notions, "it is impossible to establish any standard in revelation or even in religion." These common notions enable us to pare down all religions to their essentials and thereby eliminate many needless and divisive dogmas: "Some doctrines due to revelation may be, some of them ought to be, abandoned." Herbert's attempt to isolate the core precepts of a true religion, and his disdain for superfluous doctrines supposedly based on divine revelation, became recurring themes in later deistic writings.

Herbert spurned some common claims about religion—for example, that reason must be abandoned to make room for faith, that the church is infallible, that one should not trust one's own judgment in religious matters, that to doubt religious claims is sinful, and so forth. Such precepts, Herbert pointed out, will support false doctrines as readily as they support true doctrines:

> Now these arguments and many similar ones . . . may be equally useful to establish a false religion as to support a true one. Anything that springs from the productive, not to say seductive seed of Faith will yield a plentiful crop. What pompous charlatan can fail to impress his ragged flock with such ideas? Is there any fantastic cult which may not be proclaimed under such auspices?

According to Herbert, clergymen who "base their beliefs upon the disordered and licentious codes of superstition" are like "people who with the purpose of blinding the eyes of the wayfarer with least trouble to themselves offer with singular courtesy to act as guides on the journey." In religion as elsewhere, we should follow our own reason, not the judgments or commands of others. Indeed, God "requires every individual to render an account of his actions in the light, not of another's belief, but of his own." This call for independent judgment would become the hallmark of deism and of freethought generally.

Herbert's five common notions functioned as standards to judge alleged revelations as true or spurious, so that "the genuine dictates of Faith may rest on that foundation as a roof supported by a house." His five notions were these: (1) "There is a Supreme God." Even in polytheism, Herbert contended, a supreme god is recognized. This supreme god is blessed, the cause of all things, good, just, and wise. (2) "This Sovereign Deity ought to be Worshipped." (3) The only indispensable features of religion are virtue and piety. (4) Sins must be expiated by repentance (and, by implication, predestination is incompatible with the justice of God—a slap at Calvinism). (5) "There is Reward or Punishment after this life."

According to Herbert, if a religion does not conform to these five notions, then it is not good, nor does it provide a means to salvation. The key to salvation is moral conduct, not belief in sundry dogmas. "For how could anyone who believes more than is necessary, but who does less than he ought, be saved?"

Later deists embraced some, but not all, of Herbert's five notions. (Some deists did not believe in an afterlife, for example.) Moreover, in some respects, the later writings of John Locke, especially his empiricist theory of knowledge, exercised a far greater influence on deistic thought than Herbert ever did. Nevertheless, Herbert got the ball rolling, especially with his argument that the function of religion, first and foremost, is to serve as a guide for moral conduct. For the first several decades of the 18th century, the debate between deists and Christians was the most contentious and most widely discussed issue in England. And that debate, as we shall see, was chock-full of political implications.

7

Deism, The Age of Reason, *and Richard Carlile*

In 1730, the Anglican Bishop of London, Edmund Gibson, warned his flock to be on guard against two dangerous and heretical arguments. First was the argument that "there is not sufficient Evidence of the Truth and Authority of the Gospel-Revelation"; this convinced many people "to *reject* the Gospel" as the word of God. Second was the argument that "Reason being a sufficient Guide in Matters of Religion, there was no need of such a Revelation"; this convinced many people that they could rely on their reason alone to discern moral principles and to live a moral life without recourse to divine revelation.

Gibson was referring to the deists, and he understood their basic approach quite well. The deists believed in a God of Nature—a noninterventionist creator who lets the universe run according to natural laws without tinkering with his handiwork. Those natural laws can be known through reason, and knowledge of them (including knowledge of human nature) is both necessary *and* sufficient to guide our conduct. The derivation, elaboration, and justification of an objective moral code was seen as the essential task of a rational religion—the *religion of nature.*

Knowledge of nature, for deists, is the means by which God reveals himself to man; 18th-century deists often referred to this as *natural* revelation, or knowledge that is available to *everyone* through the use of reason. They contrasted natural revelation with *special* revelation, or knowledge supposedly communicated by God to a *particular* person or group of persons. Special revelation was often said to be "above," though not contrary to, reason, so it collided with the deistic agenda of subjecting *all* claims of knowledge to rational examination. Reason should render the final verdict in all spheres of knowledge.

Deistic reactions to special revelation ranged from skepticism to outright rejection (most typically the latter). The deists therefore undertook critical examinations of the Bible, miracles, prophecy, religious experience, and beliefs based on faith. But this aspect of deistic thought—*critical* deism, as the historian Leslie Stephen called it—was only one part of the deistic agenda. The other part, which Stephen called *constructive* deism, was to explain and defend the particular ethical precepts of the religion of nature. That meant justifying moral and political principles by reason alone, without appealing to any kind of authority, whether human or divine. And this naturalistic approach, which appealed to natural laws of human conduct, generated a good deal of skepticism about political authorities. If such authorities could not justify by rational means their claims to wield power, then they deserved neither respect nor obedience.

The deistic controversy dominated the theological and political scene in England for the first several decades of the 18th century. Many deists were among the libertarians of their day, which put them in the front line of the battle for religious and civil liberties. Deistic tracts and books elicited hundreds of replies, assailing the ideas of this troublesome movement. Orthodox rulers were especially alarmed because some prominent deists hailed from lower-class backgrounds, and they circumvented the elite intellectuals by addressing the working class directly—often ridiculing religious and political authorities in language that ordinary people could understand.

In a country with an established church, deists thus posed a serious threat to both the religious *and* political status quo. A primary purpose of the Anglican Church, for example, was to instill the virtue of passive obedience in the masses. As King Charles I said, "Religion is the only firm foundation of all power." Bishop Goodman agreed: "The church and state do mutually support and give assistance to each other." Or, in the words of another astute observer, "The state pays the clergy, and thus they have dependence upon the state."

In 1790, Edmund Burke claimed that deism had spent its force decades earlier: "Who, born within the last forty years, has read one word of Collins, and Toland, and Tindal, and Chubb, and Morgan, and that whole race who called themselves Free Thinkers? Who now reads Bolingbroke? Who ever read him through?" The freethinkers named by Burke were among the leading English deists; and it is quite true that by 1750, deism had peaked in England and that the popularity of deistic works was on the decline. But two things should be noted.

First, if the popularity of deistic works had ebbed by the later 18th century, this was partly because deism had become far less controversial, having been embraced by leading Enlightenment intellectuals, such as Adam Smith, David Hume, Edward Gibbon, Thomas Jefferson, Benjamin Franklin,

Voltaire, and many others. Proponents usually need not argue vociferously for a belief that has become part of the intellectual mainstream.

Second, with the publication of Thomas Paine's polemical defense of deism, *The Age of Reason*, in 1794 and 1795, public interest in deism picked up considerably—an interest that was fueled by vigorous governmental efforts to suppress the book. In 1819, for example, the publisher and bookseller Richard Carlile was convicted of blasphemous libel for publishing *The Age of Reason*. Carlile published the book, in part, as a test case. In his libertarian-freethought periodical, *The Republican*, he repeatedly mocked the authorities and challenged them to come and get him. The government, prodded by the Society for the Suppression of Vice, finally did precisely that. Carlile's three-day trial was closely covered by the press, and it was a fascinating trial indeed. Prominent people, including some members of Parliament, attended Carlile's trial, and thousands of commoners gathered outside the London courthouse to support their doughty champion in his battle against government censorship.

To publish anything by Thomas Paine was a hazardous enterprise, given Paine's previous conviction for seditious libel in 1792. (See my discussion of the trial in "Thomas Paine Versus Edmund Burke, Part 2."[15]) The eminent legal historian Leonard W. Levy made the following observation in his important book *Blasphemy: Verbal Offense against the Sacred, from Moses to Salman Rushdie*:

> Political radicalism, in the tradition of Paine, frequently intersected religious radicalism. A weekly newspaper demanding revocation of the stamp tax, freedom of the press, and equal voting rights most likely also preached deist doctrine, or satirized the Bible, or flirted with atheism.[16]

On the first day of his trial, Carlile read the entire text of *The Age of Reason* to the jury as part of his defense, a process that consumed nearly 12 hours. He then printed and sold the book as part of a cheap edition of the trial transcript, and in that form it was reported in Parliament to have sold 15,000 copies. Without doubt, Carlile was a clever and determined defender of civil liberties, but he paid a heavy price for those qualities. He was sentenced to two years imprisonment for publishing *The Age of Reason* and to an additional year for publishing *Principles of Nature*, a deistic work by the American freethinker Elihu Palmer. The verdict also demanded that Carlile post a bond of 1,500 pounds before his release to insure his future good conduct, but that he refused to do.

As a result, Carlile served an additional three years. Carlile entered jail a deist but emerged, six years later, an atheist; and he continued to thumb his nose at the government by selling seditious and blasphemous works.

While Carlile was imprisoned, his wife kept their bookshop going; and, because of the publicity surrounding the trial, she was able to sell thousands of copies of *The Age of Reason* within a short time. That commercial success earned Mrs. Carlile two years behind bars. She was followed by Carlile's sister, Mary Ann, who served three years. Then came a long line of employees who continued Carlile's work and suffered the same fate. Of this remarkable display of mass civil disobedience, Hypatia Bradlaugh Bonner (daughter of the prominent atheist and member of Parliament, Charles Bradlaugh) wrote the following in *Penalties upon Opinion*:

> Not only Carlile's wife and sister, but his shopmen and shopwomen, came forward to sell the condemned work, and they also were sent to prison after their leader. Volunteers came from all parts of the country to quietly fill their places, first behind the counter in the shop, next in the dock, and finally in the gaol. There were at one time as many as eight of Carlile's shopmen in Newgate under sentence for blasphemy,

in addition to the three Carliles, who lay in Dorchester Gaol, and those in the Compter and other prisons. It has been estimated that about 150 persons were imprisoned in this way. This has always seemed to me one of the most honourable and most affecting incidents in the history of the Freethought movement of the first half of the nineteenth century, those obscure men and women coming from different parts of the country, when travelling was difficult, and almost certainly in the face of the greatest opposition from family and friends, to silently offer themselves to martyrdom for the sake of an unpopular opinion. Their martyrdom was a real martyrdom, for their imprisonment was seldom for days or weeks, but usually for a year or years. The good of their fellow-men was the sole motive which inspired their heroism, even as it was their sole reward. Their action seems to have been accepted without comment as a duty performed; and so little publicity was given to their devotion that we do not even know, and I am not aware that there are any means of ascertaining, the exact number of those who actually suffered. But for all that their work was done so quietly, it was effectual, and gained that freedom for *The Age of Reason* for which they sacrificed themselves. So far as I can ascertain, since the gallant stand made by Carlile and his band of co-workers, *The Age of Reason* has never again been made the subject of prosecution in this country, although it has been sold continuously and openly up to this day.

Thus, with good reason, Leonard Levy dubbed Carlile "England's foremost blasphemer" and said that he "achieved more for the freedom of the press than any other person in the country's history."[17]

8

Miracles and Edward Gibbon

On August 10, 1787, Thomas Jefferson wrote a letter to his nephew Peter Carr in which he summarized the critical attitude toward *revealed* religion that typified the viewpoint of deists and other freethinkers of Jefferson's day. After advising Peter to "shake off all the fears and servile prejudices, under which weak minds are servilely couched," Jefferson continued,

> Fix reason firmly in her seat, and call to her tribunal every fact, every opinion. Question with boldness even the existence of God; because, if there be one, he must more approve of the homage of reason, than that of blindfold fear.

Jefferson was expressing a common deistic sentiment. If God created man with the faculty of reason, then surely he intended us to use that ability to the fullest extent possible. Of course, reason is a fallible instrument, so we are bound to make mistakes; nevertheless, it is morally better to make an honest error of judgment than to submit passively to the dictates of a religious creed because we fear the consequences of error. Deists tended to view God as a freethinker writ large. As a rational and benevolent being who endowed humans with the ability to reason so they could reach independent judgments, God would never punish his creatures for making honest mistakes—so we have nothing to fear from reasoning to the best of our ability, even if we happen to be wrong. Jefferson wrote the following:

> You will naturally examine first, the religion of your own country. Read the Bible, then, as you would read Livy or Tacitus. The facts which are within the ordinary course of nature, you will believe on the authority of the writer, as you do those of the same kind in Livy and Tacitus. The testimony of the writer weighs in their favor, in one scale, and their not being against the laws of nature, does not weigh against them. But those facts in the Bible which contradict the laws of

nature, must be examined with more care, and under a variety of faces. Here you must recur to the pretensions of the writer to inspiration from God. Examine upon what evidence his pretensions are founded, and whether that evidence is so strong, as that its falsehood would be more improbable than a change in the laws of nature, which he relates.

Jefferson cited the famous story in the Book of Joshua (10:12–13) in which God made the sun stand still "for about a whole day" so that the Israelites would have the daylight necessary to complete their slaughter of a retreating enemy. We would not believe such a story if it were related by Livy or Tacitus, but many people accept the biblical story because they believe "that the writer of that book was inspired." Jefferson advised Peter to pursue the matter further and "examine, candidly, what evidence there is of his having been inspired." Is it credible that, contrary to the laws of nature, "a body revolving on its axis, as the earth does, should have stopped, should not, by that sudden stoppage, have prostrated animals, trees, buildings, and should after a certain time have resumed its revolution, and that without a second general prostration[?] Is this arrest of the earth's motion, or the evidence which affirms it, most within the law of probabilities?"

By the time Jefferson wrote this letter, his argument against miracles (and supernatural events generally), based on an assessment of the probabilities of competing explanations, had been around for a long time and was commonly found in the writings of deists and other freethinkers. It predated by many years even the classic formulation by David Hume. One of the most influential early formulations appears in *Leviathan* (1651, chapter 32), by Thomas Hobbes. Suppose a man says that God spoke to him in a dream. According to Hobbes, this is

> no more than to say he dreamed that God spake to him; which is not of force to win belief from any man, that knows dreams are for the most part natural, and may proceed from former thoughts; and such dreams as that, from self-conceit and foolish arrogance, and false opinions of a man's own godliness, or other virtue, by which he thinks he hath merited the favour of extraordinary revelation. To say he hath seen a vision, or heard a voice, is to say, that he hath dreamed between sleeping and waking: for in such manner a man doth many times naturally take his dream for a vision, as not having observed his own slumbering. To say he speaks by supernatural inspiration, is to

say he finds an ardent desire to speak, or some strong opinion of himself, for which he can allege no natural and sufficient reason. So that though God almighty can speak to a man by dreams, visions, voice, and inspiration; yet he obliges no man to believe he hath so done to him that pretends it; who, being a man, may err, and, which is more, may lie.

The sustained skeptical attack on historical miracles, which progressed throughout the 18th century, profoundly influenced how histories were written. Even when the deist Edward Gibbon published the first volume of *The Decline and Fall of the Roman Empire* in 1776, it was still common to attribute the success of early Christianity to divine favor, or "providence." It is therefore no surprise that chapters 15 and 16 of Gibbon's great work unleashed a torrent of criticism from the orthodox, for Gibbon resolved to explain the history of early Christianity by purely naturalistic means. And in his brilliantly ironic style, Gibbon made it clear that legitimate history must preclude any and all appeals to miraculous events. If the historian substitutes miracles for explanations based on natural causation, then "history" degenerates into fabulous stories of supernatural forces that defy human understanding.

According to Gibbon, every historian who attempts to write a reliable account of early Christianity must confront the uncomfortable fact that the "scanty and suspicious materials of ecclesiastical history seldom enable us to dispel the dark cloud that hangs over the first age of the church."

> The theologian may indulge the pleasing task of describing Religion as she descended from Heaven, arrayed in her native purity. A more melancholy duty is imposed on the historian. He must discover the inevitable mixture of error and corruption which she contracted in a long residence upon earth, among a weak and degenerate race of beings.

How did Christianity come to dominate a large segment of the civilized world? A traditional answer was that this success "was owing to the convincing evidence of the doctrine itself, and to the ruling Providence of its great Author." History, however, is never that simple.

> But as truth and reason seldom find so favourable a reception in the world, and as the wisdom of Providence frequently condescends to use the passions of the human heart, and as the general circumstances of mankind, as instruments to execute its purpose,

we may still be permitted, though with becoming submission, to ask, not indeed what were the first, but what were the secondary causes of the rapid growth of the Christian church?

Gibbon attributed the eventual triumph of Christianity to five fundamental causes. But it was mainly his discussion of the third—"The miraculous powers ascribed to the primitive Church"—that generated the maelstrom of controversy: Gibbon made clear that he did not take those reported miracles seriously. He noted that reports of early Christian miracles "have been lately attacked in a very free and ingenious inquiry, which, though it has met with the most favorable reception from the public, appears to have excited a general scandal among the divines of our own as well as of the other Protestant churches of Europe." We might suppose that Gibbon was referring to David Hume's *An Enquiry Concerning Human Understanding* (1748), in which Hume repudiated all historical accounts of miracles; but Gibbon was actually thinking of a work by the Christian clergyman and scholar Conyers Middleton, *Free Inquiry into the Miraculous Powers, which Are Supposed to Have Subsisted in the Christian Church* (1749). This book, though largely forgotten today, was more widely read in the mid-18th century than Hume's account, and it generated more controversy. Indeed, it was Middleton's book that caused a young Edward Gibbon to lose what remained of his faith in Christianity.

Middleton supposedly wrote his *Free Inquiry* to defend Protestantism against Catholicism. (The qualifier "supposedly" is necessary when discussing works of this kind because rationalistic Christians sometimes joined deists in the practice of literary subterfuge.) Protestants and Catholics alike believed that miracles were a certain sign of divine favor, so Protestants needed to explain—or, more precisely, *explain away*—the many miracles reported by Catholics for centuries after the death of Jesus. The standard Protestant explanation was that miracles had declined precipitously after the apostolic age (roughly, 33–100). But in fact, as Middleton pointed out, miracles reported by Catholics remained extremely common "from the earliest father who first mentions them down to the time of the Reformation." Something was clearly amiss. Was not the Catholic Church, as viewed by Martin Luther and other Protestant Reformers, the Antichrist and the Whore of Babylon? How could the wicked Catholic Church possibly be the beneficiary of divine miracles?

Middleton sought to resolve this dilemma by focusing primarily on church fathers from the fourth century. He accused them of outright lying, of forging documents, of falsifying history, and of manufacturing other pious frauds—all in the name of winning converts to Christianity. If ever an argument exemplified the inner logic of ideas, this was it, for the question naturally arose (at least to skeptics): If miracles reported by early church fathers lacked credibility, then why wouldn't similar arguments apply to the miracles attributed to Jesus in the Gospels? Although Gibbon did not press his argument this far, at least not explicitly, one can see why his application of Middleton's critique outraged many of his orthodox readers.

According to Gibbon, our beliefs about early Christianity will be determined not so much by the arguments advanced for this or that *particular* miracle, but chiefly by "the degree of the evidence which we have accustomed ourselves to require for the proof of a miraculous event." Although the historian should not allow his religious convictions to warp his historical judgment, he must nevertheless work from a theory, whether implicit or explicit, of the relative probability of historical miracles, and then apply that theory to the particular case of early Christianity.

Gibbon, like Middleton, noted that miracles had been reported by many Christians from the earliest days of Christianity through many centuries thereafter, including the 18th century. Yet the Protestants of Gibbon's day, while persuaded of the authenticity of early miracles, were far more skeptical of later reports—especially when those reports came from Catholics—and often rejected them outright. But how can a rational line be drawn between true and false reports, between authentic miracles and superstitious fables? It was while focusing on this question that Gibbon made his most telling critique of historical miracles.

Reports of miraculous cures, which were commonplace in the early Christian community, were cited by church fathers as evidence for the truth of Christianity. But those mundane miracles should not surprise us, Gibbon argued, when we consider that "about the end of the second century, the resurrection of the dead was very far from being esteemed an uncommon event; that the miracle was frequently performed on necessary occasions . . . and that the persons thus restored to their prayers had lived afterwards among [Christians] many years." What is the historian to make of such reports? Given the frequency of reported resurrections during the second century, and given the easy availability of those former corpses who were now up and about and ready to testify for their faith, Gibbon wondered why early Christians were not able to convince many more people than they actually did. How could anyone remain skeptical about a solitary resurrection in the past (that of Jesus) when he could easily observe or otherwise verify many such resurrections in the present? Moreover, how are we to understand the curious response given by Theophilus (Bishop of Antioch) to a skeptical friend? That skeptic promised to embrace Christianity immediately upon meeting just one former corpse, but as Gibbon said, "It is somewhat remarkable that the prelate of the first Eastern church, however anxious for the conversion of his friend, thought proper to decline this fair and remarkable challenge."

Consider, observed Gibbon, that every age has its share of reported miracles, "and its testimony appears no less weighty and respectable than that of the preceding generation." How then are we to avoid inconsistency if we deny the Christian miracles of, say, the 8th or 12th centuries while accepting those in the 2nd century? There is no appreciable difference from one age to the next in the number of witnesses or in their characters, so all such miraculous accounts, in whatever era we find them, have an equal claim to our assent. Nor is there any difference in the usefulness of such miracles, for "every age had unbelievers to convince, heretics to confute, and idolatrous nations to convert; and sufficient motives might always be produced to justify the interposition of heaven."

Despite these similarities, even most friends of divine intervention believed that there was *some* period in which miracles were "either suddenly or gradually withdrawn from the Christian church." Here Gibbon was thinking primarily of

Protestants—those who affirmed the veracity of miracles during the apostolic age, using them to corroborate their own religion, while repudiating later claims of miraculous events authenticated by the despised Catholic Church.

Whatever time is chosen as marking the dividing line between authentic and bogus miracles, Gibbon called it a "just matter of surprise" that the Christians who lived during that transition period were quite unaware of the dramatic change that was taking place. Those Christians who previously had been endowed with sufficient faith to discern authentic miracles were suddenly unable to distinguish between true and false accounts, as if their faith had degenerated into superstitious credulity. Those Christians, after all, claimed to have witnessed miracles firsthand, just as they always had; and if we accept their earlier accounts (i.e., before the transition to bogus reports) as genuine, then we must suppose them to have been of sufficient discernment to recognize the marks of authentic miracles. As Gibbon put it, "The recent experience of genuine miracles should have instructed the Christian world in the ways of Providence and habituated their eye . . . to the style of the divine artist." But if this were so, then how did those discerning Christians lose the ability after the transition period and suddenly begin to defend bogus miracles with the same assurance, and using the same kind of evidence, with which they had previously confirmed authentic miracles?

Gibbon, in effect, was posing the following question: Which is more likely—that experienced, honest, and credible witnesses should suddenly and unaccountably become deceitful, unreliable, and superstitious? Or that *all* such accounts were unreliable from the outset and should not be accepted by the historian as grounds for accepting *any* historical reports of miracles? Gibbon left no doubt about his answer. The skeptical analysis of miracles—one defended by virtually every deist of the 18th century—had taken its toll, as purely secular histories became the rule rather than the exception. Although Edward Gibbon was not the first modern historian to adopt this approach—we also find it in the deists Voltaire and Adam Smith, for example—he was one of the most influential.

9

John Toland and the Nature of Reason

The Irishman John Toland (1670–1722) journeyed from Catholicism to Presbyterianism to latitudinarianism (a liberal form of Protestantism) to deism to pantheism—the latter being a word that Toland, under the influence of Spinoza's ideas, apparently coined. Having studied at the universities of Glasgow, Edinburgh, and Leyden, Toland set out to earn his way as a freelance writer and publicist for libertarian causes. Nearly 200 works and translations have been attributed to Toland; and as the historian David Berman remarked, he was "perhaps the first professional freethinker."

Modern scholars have probably devoted more attention to Toland than to any other 18th-century British freethinker, as we see in books like *John Toland and the Deist Controversy: A Study in Adaptations* (1982), by Robert E. Sullivan, and *Republican Learning: John Toland and the Crisis of Christian Culture, 1696–1722* (2003), by Justin Champion (an excellent account of Toland's political life and relationships). Toland is a major character in Margaret C. Jacob's pathbreaking study, *The Radical Enlightenment: Pantheists, Freemasons and Republicans* (1981; second revised edition, 2006); and he is discussed by Jonathan Israel in his massive, erudite volumes on the Enlightenment, including *Radical Enlightenment* (2001) and *Enlightenment Contested* (2006).

In *The Eighteenth-Century Commonwealthman* (1959), Caroline Robbins said of Toland that his "significance for the student of libertarian thought is not inconsiderable, but neither is it easy to define." Always in search of wealthy patrons who would finance his writings, Toland sometimes wrote pieces about particular political controversies that are difficult to reconcile with his basic political principles. He formed friendships with important contemporary liberals such as John Locke (who eventually severed their relationship owing to Toland's overt religious radicalism) and Lord Shaftesbury (who financed some of Toland's projects and remained friends with him throughout his life). Toland associated with various freethinkers and libertarians in Holland, which at that time was a haven for radical thinkers and printers, and those connections enabled him to reprint important 17th-century libertarian works by Milton, Harrington, Sidney, and others. In brief, to trace the life of John Toland is to undertake a fascinating tour of the leading libertarians of his day, their relationships, and clandestine literary productions. This web of relationships and underground projects largely accounts for the interest in Toland shown by modern scholars.

Toland's most important contribution to freethought and philosophy was *Christianity Not Mysterious*, published in 1696 when Toland was 26. The 19th-century historian of deism, Leslie Stephen, called Toland's book "the signal gun" of the deistic controversy that would dominate English theology for several decades. Things got off to a fiery start when the Irish Parliament ordered the book to "be publickly burnt by the hands of the Common Hangman," and further declared that Toland "be taken into the Custody of the Serjeant at Arms and be prosecuted by Mr. Attorney General, for writing and publishing said Book." In addition, "an Address should be made to the Lords Justices to give Directions that no more Copies of that Book be brought into the Kingdom, and to prevent the selling of those already imported." Toland, having no desire to play the martyr, fled Ireland to England, which was somewhat more tolerant than his native country.

The reaction by one of Toland's major critics, Peter Brown, a fellow of Trinity College in Dublin, nicely illustrates the connection that the establishment drew between criticisms of orthodox Christianity and political radicalism. Employing the standard analogy between heresy and an infectious disease, Brown wrote,

> I have no more to do here but to deliver [Toland] up into the hands of our Gouvernors. We may confute his Errours, but 'tis they only can suppress his Insolence; we only can endeavor to heal those already infected, 'tis they alone can hinder the Infection from spreading further.

Although *Christianity Not Mysterious* did not address political issues, Brown proceeded to warn against the dangerous and seditious political beliefs typically held by deists:

> How far Men in power, according to their several Stations, are obliged to intermeddle in point of Conscience, I shall not now enquire. But sure I am in point of Policy it is become no less than necessary: for the writers of this strain [i.e., deists] have given broad hints that they are as little friends to our Government, as our Religion. This Man can say that

MAGISTRATES are made for the PEOPLE, and every one knows what Doctrines of REBELLION Men are wont to insinuate by this SAYING.

In "An Apology for Mr. Toland," which was appended to later printings of his book, Toland related some options considered by members of the Irish Parliament while they were deliberating his fate:

It was moved by one that Mr. Toland himself should be burnt, and by another that he should be made to burn his Book with his own hands; and a third desir'd it should be done before the Door of the House, that he might have the pleasure of treading the Ashes under his feet.

Toland, while declining to comment in detail on the practice of burning books, noted "how fruitless this sort of proceeding has prov'd in all ages, since the Custom was first introduc'd by the *Popish Inquisitors*, who performed that Execution on the Book when they could not seize the Author whom they had destined to the Flames." The invocation of "popery" became a standard talking point for Protestant defenders of a free press after 1644, when John Milton linked censorship to Catholicism in *Areopagitica*. And Toland, like Milton, called attention to "the great Stop and Discouragement which this Practice brings to all Learning and Discoveries."

So what did Toland say in his book that so alarmed the religious and political establishment? A clue may be found in the complete title: *Christianity Not Mysterious: Or, a TREATISE Shewing, That There Is Nothing in the GOSPEL Contrary to REASON, Nor above It: And That No Christian Doctrine Can Be Properly Call'd A MYSTERY.* The title page also bears a quotation from Archbishop John Tillotson, a liberal, rationalistic Anglican who was much admired by deists: "We need not desire a better Evidence that any Man is in the wrong, than to hear him declare against Reason, and thereby acknowledg[e] that Reason is against him."

In the fashion of many deists, Toland insisted that he was a sincere Christian who wished only to purge Christianity of its irrational accretions (mysteries) and restore it to its pure, undefiled (rational) condition. Despite his protestations, Toland was widely accused of attacking Christianity, not defending it. It is difficult to say whether or not Toland was sincere, but he may have let the cat out of the bag when, in the preface, he lamented "the deplorable Condition of our Age, that a Man dares not openly and directly own what he thinks of Divine Matters." One was forced to remain silent "or to propose his Sentiments to the World by way of Paradox under a borrow'd or fictitious Name." (Toland's name did not appear in the first printing of *Christianity Not Mysterious*.) Those who had the courage to say what they really thought risked serious legal penalties. As these remarks suggest, Toland's profession of Christianity may have been a ruse to protect himself. If so, he was neither the first nor the last freethinker to employ this dodge.

Toland was firm in his commitment to reason: "I hold nothing as an Article of my Religion, but what the highest Evidence forc'd me to embrace." He refused to captivate his understanding "to any Man or Society whatsoever." Religion, as Toland saw the matter, should be reasonable, and he provided this classic statement of the freethinking deistic ideal:

> Since Religion is calculated for reasonable Creatures,
> 'tis Conviction and not Authority that should bear
> Weight with them. A wise and good Man will judg[e]
> of the Merits of a Cause consider'd only in itself,
> without any regard to Times, Places, or Persons.

Toland was unimpressed with religious scholars who flaunted their knowledge of ancient languages and declared themselves authorities to whom less educated people should defer. The "vulgar," Toland maintained, were able to assess the Bible critically and make up their own minds about its veracity, regardless of what supposed authorities told them they should believe:

> Truth is always and every where the same. And an unintelligible or absurd Proposition is never the more respected for being ancient or strange, for being originally written in Latin, Greek or Hebrew.

Contrary to some theologians, who "gravely tell us that *we must adore what we do not comprehend*," Toland insisted that everything, even revelation, must pass the test of reason or be rejected. Why? Because humans are fallible and easily deceived. Reason enables us to distinguish between fact and fancy, certainty and probability. If we abandon or ignore the dictates of reason, then we will be cast adrift in a sea of conflicting opinions (including conflicting religious opinions) with no rudder to steer our course. Questionable propositions will be accepted as axioms, old wives' fables will be mistaken for knowledge, and human impostures will be accepted as divine revelations.

Essential to Toland's case was his conception of reason, which he defined as "that Faculty of the soul which discovers the Certainty of any thing dubious or obscure, by comparing it with something evidently known." Following John Locke, Toland argued that sensory perception provides us with simple and distinct ideas, which we then compound into complex ideas. Reason is the faculty by which we perceive the agreement or disagreement of our ideas.

Like Locke, Toland said that some knowledge is self-evidently true, as we find with axioms. Strictly speaking, reason is not used in those cases because we perceive the truth of self-evident propositions immediately and without the aid of intervening ideas. But when the agreement between ideas cannot be immediately perceived, then intermediate ideas—connecting links, so to speak—are required; in those situations, reason plays an indispensable role. Reason compares a new, untested idea with an idea that is already known, thereby determining whether the new idea is consistent with our store of knowledge.

Although Toland relied heavily on Locke's epistemology, he pushed his conception of reason farther than Locke was willing to go. According to Toland, if we wish to compare ideas for their compatibility, then those ideas must be clear and distinct to begin with. Otherwise, no comparison is possible, because "when we have no Notions or Ideas of a thing, we cannot reason about it at all." Toland's theory of reason was a serious threat to venerable Christian "mysteries," such as the Trinity, because it was intrinsically hostile to truths that supposedly transcend reason. Thus, by using Locke's theory of knowledge, Toland dragged an unwilling Locke into the deistic controversy.

In 1696, Edward Stillingfleet, Bishop of Worcester, published *A Discourse in Vindication of the Trinity*. He argued that Locke's epistemology, as adapted by Toland to attack religious mysteries that transcend reason, promotes infidelity and skepticism, especially in regard to the Trinity—which was the classic example in Christianity of a doctrine that we cannot understand but must believe nonetheless. Locke, however, maintained that Toland misunderstood his theory of knowledge. Toland "made, or supposed, clear and distinct ideas necessary to certainty; but that is not my notion." Locke, it should be noted, nowhere affirmed his belief in the Trinity, and it is highly unlikely that he endorsed it; but he was a cautious man who tried to avoid public controversies over religion, so he maintained that his theory of knowledge was irrelevant to belief in the Trinity, one way or the other. But as Toland saw the matter, he was simply extending Locke's conception of reason to its logical conclusion—for how can reason compare ideas unless those ideas are clear and distinct to begin with? Indeed, Toland maintained that the nature of the human intellect is such that we cannot truly assent to a proposition unless we clearly understand its meaning:

> A man may give his verbal Assent to he knows not what, out of Fear, Superstition, Indifference, Interest,

and the like feeble and unfair Motives: but as long
as he conceives not what he believes, he cannot sin-
cerely acquiesce in it, and remains depriv'd of all solid
Satisfaction.

Faith is no help here, for we must at least understand the
meaning of a proposition before we can accept it on faith. The
Christian may claim to believe in the unintelligible, but such
a claim is meaningless verbal assent—"rash presumption and
an obstinate prejudice." The Christian may just as well claim
to believe in a *Blictri* (a traditional nonsense word):

Could that Person justly value himself upon being
wiser than his Neighbors, who having infallible
Assurance that something call'd *Blictri* had a Being
in Nature, in the mean time knew not what this
Blictri was?

Where does revelation fit into this approach? Revelation,
according to Toland, is a "means of [acquiring] information,"
not a "motive of assent." We should carefully distinguish the
method by which we acquire knowledge from the *justification*
we have to believe claims of knowledge. If a person tells us
something and expects us to believe it, then his communication must be intelligible or it signifies nothing. Suppose

this person claims to have seen a cane without two ends. We cannot believe his statement, even if we want to, because we don't know what it means. But what if this person, claiming divine inspiration, calls the peculiar cane a "mystery" that transcends reason? That would be no help, Toland argued; we still wouldn't know what he is talking about, and neither would he. Hence, "whoever reveals any thing, that is, whoever tells us something we did not know before, *his Words must be intelligible, and the Matter possible.* This Rule holds good, let God or Man be the Revealer."

According to Toland, if we are to rescue the Bible from the depths of absurdity, then we must interpret much of it figuratively; otherwise, "the highest Follies and Blasphemies may be deduc'd from the Letter of Scripture." What of those theologians who claim that a literal reading only *seems* to conflict with reason? That won't do, said Toland: "A seeming contradiction is to us as good as a real one." We cannot make sense of a contradiction, real or apparent, so it is "certainly but lost labour for us to trouble ourselves about it."

Indeed, it is impious to suggest that God, after endowing humans with the faculty of reason, would require belief in the irrational as a condition of salvation. This supposition would also breed skepticism, for if reason demands one thing while

God demands another, then we will never be certain which to follow. Toland concluded with a spirited statement of the deistic credo: "I acknowledge no ORTHODOXY but the TRUTH; and, I'm sure, wherever the TRUTH is there must also [be] the CHURCH, of God."

I have taken the time to explain Toland's basic ideas because, in addition to their inherent interest, they typify what the deists generally believed. Notably, those ideas are much less controversial today than they were in Toland's day. Toland risked his freedom and possibly his life in expressing them publicly; today, many Christians would have no serious problems with Toland's approach, even if they disagreed with his conclusions. And it is easy to see how Toland's call for conceptual clarity could be applied to the political realm, especially during an age when political authority and the demand for unconditional obedience were grounded in religious claims that were highly vulnerable to critical scrutiny.

10

The Politics of Deism

So far, this volume has covered some ideas defended by early deists and other freethinkers. I have mentioned some political implications of the deistic criticisms of orthodox Christianity but have not presented a comprehensive overview of those implications. The purpose of this chapter is to explore the politics of deism.

Many deists were in the Lockean political tradition. According to John Locke, in the state of nature (before the formation of political society), people enjoyed "natural liberty." The term referred to an anarchistic society without government, a condition of equal rights in which there is no political authority, dominion, or subordination—a society in which (in Locke's words) all "Power and Jurisdiction is reciprocal, no one having more [rights] than another." Political sovereignty, which demands that subjects obey rulers, is not a natural condition of mankind; no one is *born* with the moral authority to rule over others. Only through a process of consent can individuals alienate some of their rights by transferring them, or the power to enforce them, to a sovereign. This is done, according to Lockeans, to render the rest of our rights—especially the rights to life, liberty, and property—more secure than they would be in a state of nature.

Although Locke did not originate the notion of equal rights and liberty in a society without government—similar theoretical models had been posited by previous philosophers—it was Locke's formulation that exerted the most influence among deists and other classical-liberal freethinkers. This point is essential to understanding the hostility shown by deists to *special* revelation, in contrast to *natural* revelation. Unlike natural revelation, or the knowledge of nature acquired by the *natural* faculty of *reason*, special revelation refers to a divine communication supposedly transmitted directly from God to a *particular* person or group of persons. Thereafter, those special, inspired agents who received the divine message—commonly known as "prophets"—tell others what God supposedly told them.

Deists rejected this approach, which is found in all revealed religions (including Christianity, Judaism, and Islam). The prophet, in claiming to have received a special revelation from God, cloaks his claim of knowledge with a special cognitive status; that is to say, the prophet claims to possess knowledge that others cannot verify directly by the use of reason. Moreover, the prophet, claiming to act on God's behalf, sometimes asserts a special *political* authority over others. That assertion brings into question the doctrine of natural and equal rights, which generates a theory of government by consent, and whether it may be overridden by divine commands, as revealed through God's appointed human agent.

Consider this hypothetical situation: A self-proclaimed prophet enters a town and announces that he has been personally authorized and ordered by God to rule over that town and to punish sinners. God is angry with the inhabitants of the town, so he appointed his agent, the prophet, to communicate his displeasure and to punish sinners in his name. Skeptical Christians, having learned from the Bible about false prophets, repudiate the would-be dictator as an imposter. This hypothetical situation raises the question: By what *objective* criteria can we differentiate between true and false prophets? One sign of an authentic prophet, as traditionally accepted in Christianity, was the ability to perform miracles. (Even that sign was problematic. Leading Christian theoreticians, such as Augustine, conceded that demons and other minions of

Satan can also perform miracles.) What are the implications if a self-identified prophet is able to persuade others of his divine mission through the performance of apparent miracles? If this happens, then the prophet will have legitimized his political dominion and his *right* to punish sinners. The political right to rule will be a special, *revealed* right with divine authorization, not a *natural* right possessed by everyone. And that revealed right will *not* depend on the consent of the governed, since it was bestowed on the prophet *directly* by God, who does not require the consent of his creatures to enforce his will.

My hypothetical example—which is not all that hypothetical—illustrates the enormous political implications of special revelation. Political absolutism was typically defended by appealing to the will of God as revealed in that repository of special revelation known as the Bible. Consider, for instance, the following passage by Paul (Rom. 13:1–2, RSV), which had an incalculable impact on Christian political theory and was the pillar of defenders of unconditional obedience to an established government:

> Let every person be subject to the governing authorities. For there is no authority except from God, and those that exist have been instituted by God. Therefore

he who resists the authorities resists what God has appointed, and those who resist will incur judgment.

Now, if Paul had been viewed as a philosopher like any other philosopher, then his injunction to obey established governments would have carried no special significance. But Christians believed Paul to be a major prophet inspired by God, so his injunction was considered a divine command communicated through special revelation. In short, to disobey Paul's injunction would be to disobey the will of God.

A similar and oft-quoted passage appears in 1 Peter 2:13–14:

Be subject for the Lord's sake to every human institution, whether it be to the emperor as supreme, or to governors as sent by him to punish those who do wrong and to praise those who do right.

This passage was often invoked to justify one's duty to obey even tyrannical governments, since tyrants were sent by God to punish a sinful nation. Of course, those Christians who later defended the rights of resistance and revolution against tyrannical governments found ways around the doctrine of passive obedience. But to do so, they needed to depart from the traditional interpretation of these two biblical passages and offer their own interpretation in its place.

The likelihood of conflicting interpretations of special revelation did not pose as much of a theoretical problem for Catholics as it did for Protestants. In the Catholic Church, the
pope was the ultimate arbiter of doctrinal controversies. His
function was rather like that of the Supreme Court in American law; what the pope said was final, and that was the end
of the matter (at least in theory). But Protestants, in rejecting
papal authority and maintaining that each person should use
his or her own conscience to understand scripture, generated
a serious problem for themselves. Hundreds of Protestant
sects arose, and their conflicting interpretations of the Bible
frequently spilled over into politics. Thus, Catholic critics of
Luther, Calvin, and other Reformers were basically correct
when they predicted that the Protestant approach to the Bible
would result in a type of religious anarchy, as each individual
viewed himself as the supreme authority in religious matters.
Reverting to my previous analogy, the result was similar to
what would happen if America had no Supreme Court, or
judicial system of any kind, and every American was free to
interpret and implement law according to his own judgment.

The English deists cut through this Gordian knot by denying altogether the reasonableness of special revelation, especially if that revelation could not be verified independently
by rational means. As part of this critical project, they also

argued that it is irrational to believe in miracles—for, as noted, miracles were a sign by which a true prophet, a supposed communicator of special revelation, could allegedly be identified. Hence, the deistic assault on Christian orthodoxy was anything but pointless, random criticisms of sincere religious believers. The deists, contrary to their critics (then and now), did not wish to undermine the moral foundations of society. Rather, they aimed at profound political issues; in particular, the liberal deists wished to block the path by which defenders of political sovereignty demanded the unconditional obedience of subjects, on the basis of claims to special revelation that attempted to bypass rational justification.

The deistic agenda had many facets, but their basic attitude to special revelation and miracles is important to understand. As believers in an omnipotent, omniscient, and benevolent God of Nature, the deists did not deny the *ability* of God to communicate personally with selected individuals. Nor did deists deny the *ability* of God to perform miracles. Their criticisms (as I will discuss in subsequent chapters) were more complicated than that. For example, their typical criticism of miracles—presented most famously by David Hume— focused not on the impossibility of miracles, per se, but on the irrationality of believing *reports* of *historical* miracles. To witness an apparent miracle first-hand is one thing, but to accept the report of *another* person who *claims* to have witnessed a miracle is another thing entirely. Assessing the plausibility of historical miracles requires that we apply rational canons of historical judgment; and no historical miracle, according to the deists, can pass that test.

Since the Bible is the basis of Christianity, and since Christians accepted the Bible as a historical document that relates authentic miracles, the deistic assault on historical miracles threatened to undercut the very foundation of Christianity. To reject the authenticity of biblical miracles was to strip the Bible of its divine status and reduce it to the level of any other book. That is why Christian theologians reacted to the deistic movement with angry denunciations and vehement criticisms. Critics also understood the radical political implications of deism. If New Testament writers could not legitimately claim any special divine authority, then their theory of government and obedience, like any other political theory, required *rational* justification. If Christian rulers could not base their sovereignty on a special revelation from God, as reported in the Bible, then the Lockean theory of equal rights prevailed. No person was born with a *natural* authority or *special* rights over any other person, so Christian monarchs needed to explain and justify their supposed moral right to demand obedience from others.

Appeals to the equal rights of individuals appear in many deistic writings. Such rights cannot be overridden or nullified by a sovereign who seeks to justify his power by appealing to the Bible or other special revelation. Here is a typical passage from one of the most widely read deistic books of the 18th century, a book that elicited more than 150 replies—Matthew Tindal's *Christianity as Old as the Creation*, first published in 1730:

> Human legislators are so far from having a right to deprive their subjects of this [natural] liberty, that their main end in submitting to government is, to be protected in acting as they think fit in such cases where no one is injured; and herein the whole of human liberty consists, the contrary being a state of mere vassalage; and men are more or less miserable, according as they are more or less deprived of this liberty; especially in matters of mere religion, wherein they ought to be most free.

The liberal deists attempted to safeguard the equal rights of individuals by discrediting all appeals to special revelation that sought to do an end run around natural rights and thereby justify political dominion over unwilling subjects. Of course, the deists knew that many orthodox Christians valued freedom and had no desire to use special revelation for nefarious political purposes. But the liberal deists also understood that freedom requires more than good intentions. They believed that a major Christian theory that had been used to justify despotism in the name of God should be dissected and refuted, point by point. This critical project, through detailed analyses of special revelation and miracles, resulted in the outright repudiation of anyone who claimed to possess special rights bestowed by God.

11

Skepticism

In 1562, the French printer Henri Estienne published the first Latin edition of *Outlines of Pyrrhonism*, written c. 200 by the Greek physician Sextus Empiricus. Estienne explained that the work by Sextus had taught him that we cannot rely on reason, a fallible and unreliable instrument, in matters of religion, because it will only pave the way for atheism. Seven years later, another publisher of Sextus, the French Catholic Gentian Hervet, also maintained that the arguments of Pyrrhonic skepticism, as summarized by Sextus, could be used to defend Christianity.

Pyrrhonic skepticism is named after Pyrrho of Elis (c. 315–275 BCE), an obscure figure who is portrayed in secondary accounts as a complete doubter, especially in ethical matters. Rather than endure the mental anguish that comes from seeking certain knowledge, Pyrrho is said to have suspended judgment, thereby attaining the mental state known to Greek philosophers as *ataraxia*, or what today we would call contentment, or peace of mind. Pyrrho's ideas were put into systematic form by Aenesidemus (c. 100–40 BCE), and it was Aenesidemus and his followers who first embraced the label "skeptic" (from *skeptikos*, meaning "thoughtful" or "doubter").

Pyrrhonic skepticism should be distinguished from another type of skepticism that also originated in ancient Greece. Known as Academic skepticism, this school derived its name from Plato's Academy and was inspired by a remark attributed to Socrates: "All I know is that I know nothing." As formulated by Arcesilaus (c. 315–241 BCE) and Carneades (c. 213–129 BCE), Academic skepticism maintained that we can attain various degrees of probability, but never certainty, in our quest for knowledge. This position was based on the standard Greek distinction between knowledge (*episteme*) and opinion (*doxa*). In this scheme, if a proposition might be false, then it cannot be certain and is therefore mere opinion, not knowledge. Since both our senses and our reason are unreliable to some degree, we can never lay claim to absolute truth, or real knowledge. And since nothing can be known with certainty, we must rely instead on opinions that vary in their degrees of probability.

Pyrrhonic skeptics criticized Academic skepticism as dogmatic. The Academics were not true skeptics because they claimed to know with certainty that certainty is impossible—a claim that is self-contradictory and therefore self-refuting. The Pyrrhonists, in contrast, did not claim that knowledge is impossible; rather, they suspended judgment on all such theoretical questions, thereby avoiding the mental discomfort generated by taxing one's brain with insoluble problems. For the Pyrrhonists, skepticism was a mental attitude and a way of life, not merely an abstract philosophical doctrine. They refused to judge or to criticize the laws and customs of their society, resolving instead to accept things as they appear to be, without committing themselves to any unorthodox position. In that way, they hoped to attain the mental tranquility of *ataraxia*.

Of these two schools of skepticism, it was Pyrrhonic skepticism that was destined to exert the most influence on the course of Western philosophy—perhaps because no major writings of the Academics survived the ravages of time. What we know of Academic arguments was transmitted through much later secondary accounts, such as those of Cicero and Augustine. The Pyrrhonists were more fortunate, owing to the summary written by Sextus Empiricus, *Outlines of Pyrrhonism*. Manuscript copies of that work began to circulate during the Italian Renaissance and were eventually disseminated throughout Europe.

Pyrrhonic skepticism, as summarized by Sextus, created a sensation—some called it a crisis—among European intellectuals. Some philosophers (such as Michel de Montaigne) embraced it enthusiastically, whereas others (such as René Descartes) attempted with equal enthusiasm to refute it. But the influence of Sextus Empiricus was so tremendous that by the end of the 17th century, the "divine Sextus" was widely hailed as the father of modern philosophy.[18] Pyrrhonism would remain a serious topic of discussion in Enlightenment philosophy, as we see in the writings of David Hume.

The writings of Sextus Empiricus were used mainly by French Catholics to defend a position known as *fideism*, which is essentially an effort to vindicate faith at the expense of reason. By stripping reason of its cognitive efficacy, the fideists appealed to faith as the sole and ultimate source of certainty. If we look to reason instead, we will sink into a morass of uncertainty where no belief can claim superiority over any other. Fideism was a popular method of argument among French Catholics for three-quarters of a century, one that was commonly aimed at Calvinists. Pyrrhonic skepticism also proved useful among theologians, both Catholic and Protestant, against freethinkers who sought to discredit Christian doctrines in the name of reason. By demonstrating the impotence of reason, Pyrrhonism teaches us intellectual humility and prepares us to receive the doctrines of Christ through faith.

As noted above, Pyrrhonic skepticism, unlike Academic skepticism, did not deny outright the possibility of certain knowledge; Pyrrhonists argued instead that to affirm that certainty is unattainable is to take an inherently uncertain position. When examining a philosophic belief, the Pyrrhonists marshaled a battery of arguments for both sides, pro and con, in an effort to show that reason cannot justify one belief more than another. Given this dialectical standoff, the Pyrrhonists argued that we should disengage ourselves from useless philosophic controversies. Only in this way can we attain peace of mind.

Pyrrhonic skepticism was inherently conservative, which explains much of its appeal to those Catholics who were attempting to defend the authority of their church against Protestant criticisms. According to the Pyrrhonists, rather than engaging in futile speculations about philosophic truth—which could be used to criticize the religious and political status quo—we should resolve to accept things as they appear to be, without attempting to judge them. That means we should passively submit to the laws, customs, and traditional beliefs of our society, rather than challenging them with philosophic principles that cannot themselves be justified.

This conservative bias is what made Pyrrhonism so useful to Catholics during the Counter Reformation. Pyrrhonic arguments, when directed against freethinkers and unbelievers, could be (and were) used by Catholics and Protestants alike, as a means of showing the superiority of faith over reason. But in the internecine battle between Catholics and Protestants, the conservative implications of Pyrrhonism proved to be of greater utility to the former. Protestants, after all, were the innovators—the radicals who had rejected the traditional authority of the Church, root and branch. And though Protestants did not seek to replace that authority with reason, they did appeal to personal judgment in biblical matters as the ultimate rule of faith.

The Catholic Pyrrhonists predicted that dire consequences would result from this religious individualism. The Protestants, in counseling people to rely on their own judgment in religious matters rather than on the authority of the church, had embarked on a dangerous path. The feeble and unreliable judgments of individuals would result in diverse and conflicting religious beliefs and end in atheism.

Montaigne (1533–1592), the major proponent of Catholic Pyrrhonism, put it this way:

> The mass of ordinary people lack the faculty of judging things as they are, letting themselves be carried away by chance appearances. Once you have put into their hands the foolhardiness of despising and criticizing opinions which they used to hold in the highest awe (such as those which concern their salvation), and once you have thrown into the balance of doubt and uncertainty any articles of their religion, they soon cast all the rest of their beliefs into similar uncertainty. They had no more authority for them, no more foundation, than for those you have just undermined; and so, as though it were the yoke of a tyrant, they shake off all those other concepts which had been impressed upon them by the authority of Law and the awesomeness of ancient custom. . . . They then take it upon themselves to accept nothing on which they have not pronounced their own approval, subjecting it to their individual assent.

Montaigne applied Pyrrhonic skepticism to the great theological question of his day: What is the proper rule of faith? By what criterion should we assess religious claims and accept one scriptural interpretation over others? In this area as in others, according to Montaigne, reason cannot bring us to definitive conclusions. And if reason cannot discern the rule of faith, then relying on reason in this sphere will land us in such doubt that it will be fatal to Christian belief. The only alternative is to accept tradition—that is, to submit to the authority of the Catholic Church.

Montaigne is one of the most ambiguous figures in modern thought. Was he a sincere defender of the Catholic faith, or was his fideism merely a smokescreen for disbelief? That question, debated for centuries, has become a cottage industry for philosophers and historians of the Counter Reformation. On the one hand, for example, the Montaigne scholar M. A. Screech presents Montaigne as a sincere Catholic who should be taken at his word. On the other hand, Richard Popkin, while conceding that Montaigne (and other fideists) "seem capable of both a religious and non-religious interpretation," hazards the opinion that "at best, Montaigne was probably mildly religious. His attitude appears to be more that of indifference or unexcited acceptance, without any serious religious experience or involvement."

Whatever Montaigne's own views may have been, his writings (especially "An Apology for Raymond Sebond," the longest section in his *Essays*) provided a mine of information and arguments for later generations of freethinkers—who, as Screech put it, "pillaged [the 'Apology'] for anti-Christian arguments." Pyrrhonism was clearly a double-edged sword that could be used either to defend Christianity or to attack it. This point was not lost on Catholic authorities, who, in 1697, placed Montaigne's *Essays* on the Index of Prohibited Books.

12

Francis Bacon and the Rise of Secularism

In the previous chapter, I discussed the influence of Pyrrhonic skepticism on modern thought and the ways in which skeptical arguments were used to support the fideistic contention that reason cannot generate certainty, leaving us no choice in religious matters except to rely entirely on faith. Among the important consequences of Pyrrhonism were the replies it evoked from philosophers who attempted to refute it. Two of the most important attempts were undertaken by René Descartes (1596–1650) and Francis Bacon (1561–1626). In this chapter, I focus on the arguments of Bacon, who was a seminal figure in the development of modern secularism.

It is difficult to imagine the course that modern philosophy might have taken if René Descartes and Francis Bacon had never existed. Both are widely recognized as key figures in the history of modern philosophy. Descartes is often credited as the founding father of the philosophical trend known as Rationalism. Bacon, if not credited as the father of modern Empiricism (an honor usually reserved for John Locke), has at least attained the status of its godfather. And Bacon's extraordinary importance as a philosopher of science has long been appreciated.

Although Bacon was accused of being a secret atheist, his belief in Christianity, though extremely liberal by the standards of his day, appears to have been sincere. He flatly rejected a literal interpretation of the Bible in favor of doctrinal pluralism, maintaining that biblical passages should serve as "infinite springs and streams of doctrines." Because biblical writers typically expressed themselves through metaphor, scripture should not be used as a source of scientific knowledge, nor should it serve as a basis to criticize the conclusions of science. The spheres of religion and science should be kept completely separate, neither being allowed to impinge on the domain of the other. The various "mysteries" of Christian revelation, such as the Trinity, are incomprehensible to reason and therefore must be accepted entirely on faith.

When theology is permitted to transgress beyond its proper sphere, "every development of philosophy, every new frontier and direction, is regarded by religion with unworthy suspicion and violent contempt." Thus, as Peter Urbach (*Francis Bacon's Philosophy of Science: An Account and a Reappraisal,* 1987) observed, Bacon "banished the Bible as a source of information for the scientist."

In driving a wedge between philosophy and theology by insisting that we "give to faith only that which is faith's," Bacon gave his blessing to a secular tendency that, like a slow-acting poison, would eventually undercut the foundations of orthodox Christianity. As Franklin Baumer, commenting on the rise of 17th-century secularism, explained in *Modern European Thought: Continuity and Change in Ideas, 1600–1950,*

> Secularism, unlike free thought, posed no threat to particular theological tenets. What it did was to out-flank theology by staking out autonomous spheres of thought. The tendency was, more and more, to limit theology to the comparatively restricted sphere of faith and morals.

Bacon's scientific secularism, while it did not challenge Christianity, per se, exiled God to the nether regions of faith and theology, thereby denying him any direct role in the acquisition of natural knowledge. "God," according to Bacon, "worketh nothing in nature but by second causes." Speaking of God as the *first* cause is a matter of theology, not science, and reasonable men "do not unwisely mingle or confound these learnings together." Bacon's secularism was so consistent that he rudely dismissed any reference to miracles in accounts of natural science and history: "As for the narrations touching the prodigies and miracles of religions, they are either not true, or not natural; and therefore impertinent for the story of nature."

It is fair to say that Bacon had more influence on the rise of secularism than did Descartes, who assigned to God a key role in his philosophical system. Far more significant, however, is the substantial difference in their views of human reason (or "understanding," as Bacon, Locke, and others in their tradition often called it). In a nutshell, we may say that for Descartes, reason is an infallible faculty of cognition, an instrument that cannot fail in its quest for absolute certainty if used properly. For Bacon, in contrast, reason is inherently fallible; it is prone to error even in the best of circumstances, so we must stand perpetually on guard, willing to correct or revise our present beliefs.

Both Bacon and Descartes rejected the epistemological skepticism of Montaigne and other fideists—according to whom we must rely on faith to attain a certainty that reason is unable to provide. But their approaches differed significantly. Bacon, unlike Descartes, did not attempt to overthrow skepticism with a definitive theoretical refutation; he did not employ the Cartesian method of systematic doubt in an effort to establish an infallible criterion of knowledge, such as the intuitive grasp of clear and distinct ideas. Instead, Bacon plotted a course to certainty that must be traveled step by step, and he insisted that we must sometimes traverse the same ground over and over again to check our bearings. Certainty, in other words, does not reveal itself to reason in a flash of insight; rather, it is an elusive ideal that reason may attain to a greater or lesser extent, depending on the circumstances.

As Bacon saw the matter, the skeptical argument that we can never achieve certainty amounts to little more than a pretentious bit of futile and self-defeating dogmatism. The skeptic, having proclaimed that infallible certainty is unattainable, never tries to attain it because he knows that man is a fallible being for whom error is an ever-present possibility. Bacon responded, in effect, that defining "certainty" in terms of infallibility makes certainty unattainable to human beings at the outset and thereby renders the concept of certainty altogether irrelevant to human knowledge. Rather than blocking

the path to knowledge with an arbitrary and unrealistic defi-
nition of "certainty," we should recognize that the quest for
knowledge is beset with difficulties; then, through a process
of trial and error, we should see whether those difficulties can
be overcome. Bacon wrote,

> Our method and that of the skeptics agree in some
> respects at first setting out, but differ most widely,
> and are completely opposed to each other in their
> conclusions; for they roundly assert that nothing can
> be known; we, that but a small part of nature can
> be known, by the present method; their next step,
> however, is to destroy the authority of the senses and
> understanding, whilst we invent and supply them
> with assistance.

Bacon's attack on skepticism distinguished *particular* doubt
from *total* doubt. "Particular doubt"—that is, doubt that
arises in regard to a *specific* knowledge claim—is useful both
as a spur to inquiry and as an antidote to the proliferation of
error, as when a false conclusion is inferred from a premise
that has not been sufficiently justified. "Total doubt," in contrast, is the *universal* doubt of skepticism. Bacon regarded the
latter as a rather cowardly surrender to the difficulties that
frequently arise in our quest for knowledge.

Skeptics sometimes pointed to the diversity of philosophic opinions to support their contention that certainty is unattainable, but Bacon was unconvinced. Nature is far more complex than the mind of man, so the same essential truth may be expressed in different ways by different thinkers. Scientific knowledge, cumulative and open-ended, progresses as one scientist improves on the contributions of his predecessors. Human intellect is not an infallible instrument—far from it; but to say that an instrument can *sometimes* fail is not to say that it must *necessarily* fail in *every* case. Just as the human hand could not construct architectural wonders without the aid of external tools, so the human intellect cannot attain certainty without the aid of objective methods to test and validate our knowledge claims. Again quoting Bacon,

> The unassisted hand and the understanding left to itself possess but little power. Effects are produced by the means of instruments and helps, which the understanding requires no less than the hand; and as instruments either promote or regulate the motion of the hand, so those that are applied to the mind prompt or protect the understanding.

The skeptic who denies that we can ever attain certainty is like a person who, after observing the limited power of the naked hand, declares that man will never be able to build a cathedral. The skeptic, trapped in a sophistical web of his own making, perpetually whines about the obstacles to knowledge. Bacon argued that the time of the philosopher would be better spent devising methods—cognitive instruments, in effect—to enable us to overcome those obstacles.

Thus, if Bacon's stress on the inherent fallibility of reason did not land him in skepticism, it is because he rejected infallibility as a criterion of certainty. Certainty is something we achieve through sustained mental effort, a laborious and systematic process of trial and error, not something that is revealed to us in a flash of infallible insight. Certainty is achieved piecemeal through the investigation of particular knowledge claims, not wholesale through a process of deductive reasoning based on clear and distinct ideas. Our ideas, if they are to generate useful knowledge, must be framed according to our experience of nature; and that experience, if it is to be reliable, must be subjected to objective methods of verification.

The foregoing must be kept in mind if we are to appreciate Bacon's celebrated discussion of "idols," or "fallacies of the mind of man," that hinder our quest for knowledge. Bacon was the first great pathologist of human reason. Later philosophers used his mode of analysis—a mixture of psychology, sociology, and epistemology—to explain why reasonable people with good intentions can, and often do, hold incompatible beliefs. It was largely owing to Bacon that religious dissent, which had previously been condemned as the deliberate (and therefore sinful) rejection of divine truth, came to be regarded as the innocent byproduct of human fallibility. This doctrine of the natural diversity of opinion (especially as developed by John Locke) was destined to play a key role in the struggle for religious toleration.

Bacon's basic point is quite simple and, from the perspective of a Cartesian rationalist, quite disturbing: There is no natural harmony or correspondence between the world of ideas and the world of nature. If, as the rationalist maintains, our senses are inherently untrustworthy and liable to lead us astray, the same is true of reason itself. The human intellect has its own distinctive characteristics, a nature apart from that which it seeks to know. Understanding is not a passive process in which the intellect merely reflects the external world of nature. Rather, the intellect actively contributes to the cognitive process, leaving indelible marks on its final product. Thus, "the human mind resembles those uneven mirrors which impart their own properties to different objects, from which rays are emitted and distort and disfigure them." Bacon calls these natural distortions "idols," or false notions, of the human understanding.

Bacon divided his idols into four principal categories: (1) Idols of the Tribe "are inherent in human nature and the very tribe or race of man." (2) Idols of the Cave pertain to the individual, for "everybody (in addition to the errors common to the race of man) has his own individual den or cavern, which intercepts and corrupts the light of nature." (3) Idols of the Market are "formed from the commerce and association of men with each other." (4) Idols of the Theater "have crept into men's minds from the various dogmas of peculiar systems of philosophy . . . as so many plays brought out and performed, creating fictitious and theatrical worlds."

Human understanding, according to Bacon, does not operate in isolation apart from the will and affections. Our desires and feelings influence how we think. We are more likely to believe something that we wish were true, the comfortable and the familiar, rather than something difficult, disturbing, or unconventional. We also tend to develop a vested interest in our beliefs, defending a pet theory because we created it or worked hard on it, or simply because of its familiarity.

Bacon maintained that people who think differently often exhibit different biases. People with strong powers of observation, for example, may attribute too much importance to minor differences among things; other people may overemphasize their similarities. In any case, examining our own beliefs objectively is extremely difficult, given the many subjective factors that affect our understanding. But Bacon offered a valuable piece of advice—namely, that we should be particularly suspicious of those theories that give us the most satisfaction and should subject them to rigorous scrutiny and criticism.

Perhaps the most radical aspect of Bacon's approach was his unequivocal rejection of "final causation" as a legitimate mode of explanation in the physical sciences. To appeal to a final cause is to explain a phenomenon in terms of its supposed purpose; and though Bacon's critique of this method was primarily directed at the Aristotelians of his day—known as "scholastics" (i.e., "schoolmen") because of their dominant presence in European universities—it had far broader implications for the Christian worldview. To banish final causation from the realm of explanation is to banish all references to a divine purpose in the universe. Bacon made God an absentee architect of creation—a first cause who, having created the universe, thereafter left it alone to operate according to the secondary causes of natural law. Understandably, Bacon was universally praised by later deists.

Indeed, depending on how we read Bacon, he may even have rejected the notion of a first cause altogether. According to Bacon, we cannot reasonably demand an explanation for existence, because something must first exist before it can function as a cause of something else. So why do so many people seek to go beyond the brute fact of existence and posit God as a first cause? Because, said Bacon, the human mind is active and restless; it is engaged in a perpetual quest for intelligibility, for ultimate explanations that will satisfy its desire to understand. But when reason is unable to satisfy that metaphysical urge, as is often the case, the imagination steps in with fanciful explanations of its own.

Thus, the mind moves up the ladder of cause and effect and posits God as the ultimate cause of everything else. This is a fancy of the imagination, not a judgment of the understanding. Reason tells us that "the greatest generalities in nature," such as the fact of existence, must be accepted "just as they are found" and that such facts are "not causable." Existence, in other words, is a causal primary, the ultimate foundation on which all explanations depend, an irreducible fact beyond which the mind cannot go. But the mind does not want to hear that reasoning; it cannot find satisfaction in being told that its metaphysical journey must end, abruptly and unceremoniously, at the impenetrable wall of existence. Thus, the imagination satisfies this metaphysical desire at the expense of reason, and another idol takes its toll.

13

Benedict Spinoza

In 1656, Baruch Spinoza (1632–1677), a brilliant and heretical young Dutch scholar descended from Portuguese Jews, was excommunicated and anathematized by the elders of the Amsterdam Synagogue. Spinoza changed his name to Benedict (the Latin equivalent of Baruch) and thereafter made a modest living as a lens grinder. In 1673, Spinoza turned down the chair of philosophy at the University of Heidelberg, fearing that the position might compromise his intellectual independence. Spinoza published only two works during his lifetime. The first, an exposition of the philosophy of Descartes, was relatively uncontroversial; but the second—the *Theologico-Political Treatise*, published anonymously in 1670 under the imprint of a fictitious printer—was a bombshell. In the words of Richard Popkin (*The History of Scepticism from Erasmus to Descartes,* rev. ed., 1979), it "is a devastating critique of revealed knowledge claims, which has had an amazing effect over the last three centuries in secularizing modern man."

Although Spinoza completed his celebrated work on metaphysics, *The Ethics*, in 1674, he declined to have it published because of the outrage it would almost certainly provoke. Published shortly after Spinoza's death, the book had precisely that effect. *The Ethics*, though highly abstract and often difficult to follow, earned Spinoza dubious fame as the leading European atheist; for many decades thereafter, being called a "Spinozist" was tantamount to being called an atheist. In his lengthy article on Spinoza in the *Historical and Critical Dictionary*, a massive work that greatly influenced Enlightenment thought, Pierre Bayle (1647–1706)—a notorious skeptic in his own right—called Spinoza "a systematic atheist" who made use of equivocation and artifice "to avoid showing his atheism plainly." The *Theologico-Political Treatise* is "a pernicious and detestable book in which he slips in all the seeds of atheism," so his followers "have hardly any religion at all." Friends reported that, though Spinoza died "completely convinced of his atheism," he had avoided the label because "he wished not to give his name to a sect." Bayle continued,

> Very few persons are suspected of adhering to his theory; and among those who are suspected of it,

there are few who have studied it; and among the latter group, there are few who have understood it and have not been discouraged by the perplexities and the impenetrable abstractions that are found in it.

Bayle regarded Spinoza as an atheist for the same reason that occurs to most readers: While praising God to the hilt as a necessary and infinitely perfect being who is the cause of all things, Spinoza explicitly identified "God" with "nature." He expressly denied the existence of a transcendent being—that is, a being that exists apart from nature and acts on it as an external agent. Every change that occurs, every instance of cause and effect, is immanent within nature and takes place according to the deterministic laws of nature.

Scholars continue to debate whether Spinoza was really an atheist; and if this debate cannot be resolved, the fault lies partly in the term itself: "atheist" is rarely used in a clear and consistent manner. Spinoza once remarked, "my opinion concerning God differs widely from that which is ordinarily defended by Christians and other theists. For I hold that God is of all things the cause immanent," and "I do not bring in the idea of God as a judge." Nature, according to Spinoza, "is the power of God under another name"; "in nature there is no substance save God, nor any modifications save those which are in God." As for the attributes of God, "By *eternity*,

I mean existence itself"; "*reality* and *perfection* I use as synonymous terms"; "infinite" means that "the nature of the universe is not limited," that it is "infinitely modified, and compelled to undergo infinite variations." Moreover, "God does not act according to freedom of the will" but is determined by the eternal laws of his own nature. To suppose that God can intervene in the natural course of events through miracles is absurd: "I have taken miracles and ignorance as equivalent terms." "God can never decree, or never could have decreed anything but what is," nor does God act "with a view of promoting what is good."

In short, Spinoza's God is neither supernatural nor transcendent; he does not intervene in human affairs or "act" in any meaningful sense at all. The God of Spinoza bears virtually no resemblance to what most people mean by "God." He is a prime example of what Blaise Pascal contemptuously referred to as the metaphysical God of the philosophers, in contrast to the personal God of religion.

Although Spinoza did not believe that God should be the object of religious worship or prayer, he did exhibit a profound reverence for this perfect being (while also noting that all of nature is inherently perfect). One observer even called him "God-intoxicated." But we should keep in mind that Spinoza regarded truth and reality as two sides of the same coin; when he contended that lasting happiness can only come from the contemplation of God, it appears he was advocating nothing more than the pursuit of wisdom—a quest for universal knowledge that is certain, immutable, and eternal—that has captivated western philosophers for 2,500 years. Indeed, in that respect, Spinoza differed little from Aristotle, who also touted the contemplative life of the philosopher as the most desirable, and who labeled as "divine" our metaphysical knowledge of first principles.

Spinoza's influence on later deists can be difficult to establish from their writings. Spinoza's reputation as an atheist made him a dangerous precedent to cite, especially for those deists who sought to distance themselves from that odious label. Voltaire, the leading Enlightenment deist, viewed Spinoza's atheistic ideas with disdain and criticized them vehemently. But here we should distinguish between Spinoza's critical assault on revealed religion, as expressed in the *Theologico-Political Treatise*, and his positive metaphysical theories, as expressed in *The Ethics*. Many deists, even if they failed to mention Spinoza by name, clearly drew from his criticisms of the Bible and miracles; his metaphysical views had far less influence on later generations of freethinkers. A notable exception was John Toland, who, though critical of Spinoza in some respects, coined and embraced the label "pantheist" to describe a person whose conception of God was very similar to Spinoza's. Although Toland insisted that pantheists are not atheists, to many of his readers this appeared a distinction without a difference. (See my discussion of Toland in chapter 9.)

From a theological perspective, the most troublesome part of Spinoza's *Ethics* is the appendix to Part One. Although this section specifically targets final causes, or purposes, in nature, it also qualifies as the most sustained criticism of the "design argument" in early modern philosophy. The design argument, long considered the most persuasive proof for the existence of God, prevented many 18th-century deists from taking the plunge into atheism. The design argument was defended by some of the most celebrated names in the history of science and freethought, such as Isaac Newton, Voltaire, and Thomas Paine; it continued to be immensely popular well into the 19th century, until the Darwinian theory of evolution provided a naturalistic explanation for the complex, adaptive, and seemingly purposive nature of life.

According to Spinoza, we have a natural desire to understand the causes of natural phenomena (especially those that influence our welfare), and we also have a natural tendency to view nature in human terms. Thus, when we lack knowledge of natural causes, our imagination fills the void by attributing to nature the same kind of purposes and intentions that we observe in ourselves and other human beings. A kind of metaphysical transference is at work here. Many events and things affect us for good or ill. They are important to us, so we assume they were brought about with us in mind, by a being to whom *we* are important. We think that the world was specially created for our benefit and that its complex structure and immense beauty must have been designed by a purposeful, powerful, and intelligent being.

The first problem with this theory, Spinoza contended, is that "it does away with the perfection of God; for, if God acts for an object, he necessarily desires something which he lacks." Some theologians tried to get around this problem (which had been proposed by some skeptics of ancient Greece) by stipulating that God created the world for his own sake, not for the sake of his creation. But that reply (or any similar to it) is unsatisfactory; it still implies that God—a perfect being who lacks nothing and therefore can desire nothing—"lacked those things for whose attainment he created means, and further that he desired them." (An interesting side note is that Ludwig von Mises repeated this argument in *Human Action*.)

To ascribe purpose to nature is essentially an argument from ignorance, according to Spinoza. Nature is infinitely complex, so we can never claim to *know* that a given phenomenon could not have been produced by natural causes. So, rather than attempt the impossible, rather than attempt to prove that a natural cause is impossible in a given case, theologians appeal to ignorance instead. Theologians attribute what we don't presently understand, or what science has failed to explain, to God—a "sanctuary of ignorance" that satisfies the imagination but not the understanding. Quoting Spinoza,

> If a stone falls from a roof on to someone's head, and kills him, [theologians] will demonstrate by their new method, that the stone fell in order to kill the man; for, if it had not by God's will fallen with that object, how could so many circumstances (and there are often many concurrent circumstances) have all happened together by chance? Perhaps you will answer that the event is due to the facts that the wind was blowing, and the man was walking that way. "But why," they will insist, "was the wind blowing, and why was the man at that very time walking that way?" If you again answer, that the wind had then sprung up because the sea had begun to be agitated the day before, the weather being previously calm, and that the man had been invited by a friend, they will again insist: "But why was the sea agitated, and

why was the man invited at that time?" So they would pursue their questions from cause to cause, till at last you take refuge in the will of God—in other words, the sanctuary of ignorance.

Similarly, those who do not understand how nature could have produced the human body will often "conclude that it has been fashioned, not mechanically, but by divine and supernatural skill." And "anyone who seeks for the true causes of miracles, and strives to understand natural phenomena as an intelligent being, and not to gaze at them like a fool, is set down and denounced as an impious heretic."

Spinoza's use of the term "miracle" in the latter passage is highly significant. The design argument is ultimately an appeal to miraculous causes—causes that do not, and cannot, occur in the natural course of events. Thus, an "explanation" via design is not a legitimate alternative to scientific and other naturalistic explanations. To refer to a miraculous "cause" is to refer to something that is inherently unknowable, and this "sanctuary of ignorance" explains nothing at all. However much it may soothe the imagination of the ignorant, it does nothing to satisfy the *understanding* of a rational person.

Another feat of the imagination is to "firmly believe that there is an *order* in things," and that things which further this order are metaphysically "good." Spinoza's objection to this view is perhaps the most radical part of his critique, for even atheists often speak of an order inherent in nature. Spinoza disagreed. Nature is what it is, and things behave as they do by virtue of what they are. Nature exhibits neither order nor chaos, neither good nor evil, neither beauty nor deformity; these and similar assessments are derived from human standards, not from nature, per se. We consider a natural phenomenon "well-ordered" when it can be easily understood or when it affects us favorably, whereas we speak of "confusion" (or "chance" or "chaos") when confronted with a phenomenon that eludes our understanding or brings unforeseen evils upon us.

In thus relegating "order" to the same status as "beauty" and other subjective evaluations, Spinoza cut off the design argument at its roots. If the fundamental facts of nature—their ultimate explanation, so to speak—are that things exist, that things are what they are, and that things behave as they do by virtue of what they are, then to attribute "order" to natural phenomena is simply to restate the fundamental facts in an abbreviated form. That is to say, the fundamental facts are comprehensible. If, however, we wish to say something more—if by "order" we mean that nature exhibits beauty, harmony, goodness, or the like—then we are merely importing additional evaluations into our set of fundamental facts. That means we need only explain those evaluations, not the facts they purport to describe.

Hence, according to Spinoza, if we wish to explain the "purpose" and "design" in nature, we need only look within ourselves, to the reasons and causes that generate these evaluations. It is as unnecessary as it is absurd to posit the existence of an unknowable cause (God) who uses unknowable means (miracles) to bring about results that no perfect being—no being with unfulfilled wants—could possibly desire. Spinoza concluded,

> All the explanations commonly given of nature are mere modes of imagining, and do not indicate the true nature of anything, but only the constitution of the imagination; and, although they have names, as though they were entities, existing externally to the imagination, I call them entities imaginary rather than real; and, therefore, all arguments against us drawn from such abstractions are easily rebutted.

In this chapter, I have sketched some of Spinoza's ideas about God and religion. In the next chapter, I discuss some of his important insights about freedom of conscience and social diversity.

14

Spinoza on the Bible

Among contemporary scholars, no one has stressed the influence and historical significance of Benedict Spinoza more than has Jonathan Israel, especially in two of his formidable books: *Radical Enlightenment*[19] and *Enlightenment Contested.*[20] Israel noted in the latter volume that Spinoza's infamous reputation prevented many thinkers from acknowledging their intellectual debts to him. Furthermore,

> No one else, not even Hobbes, was denounced as often as Spinoza whether in the late seventeenth, early eighteenth, or mid eighteenth century, or in so many countries; or indeed was so widely known to the public as a universal philosophical bogeyman. In this respect . . . , Spinoza remained the most feared

philosopher in eighteenth-century Europe, eclipsing in contemporary perception every other alleged "atheist" in history.

The result was spreading awareness, discussion, refutation, condemnation, and . . . also admiration of Spinoza often without his name being so much as mentioned.[21]

Both of Spinoza's major works, the *Theologico-Political Treatise* (1670) and the posthumously published *Ethics*, were widely excoriated as atheistic and politically subversive. Between the two, it was the *Treatise* that exerted the most influence on later generations of freethinkers. In the *Treatise*—a pioneering work in what later would be called "higher criticism" of the Bible—Spinoza insisted that we should approach the Bible as we would any other historical book (or, in this case, collection of books). We should not begin with the assumption that the Bible is divinely inspired and then afford it special treatment when we encounter stories that we would reject in any other history. Rather, we should examine biblical accounts with the same rational objectivity and critical attitude that we would apply to any other book.

As a result, Spinoza analyzed the Bible with a boldness that had rarely if ever been seen before. He provided an abundance of details to support his claim that the Bible is "faulty, mutilated, tampered with, and inconsistent." We don't know the authors, circumstances, or dates of many biblical books. Moreover, "we cannot say into what hands they fell, nor how the numerous varying versions originated; nor, lastly, whether there were other versions, now lost."

Spinoza drew on various sources for his critique of the Bible. He credited Abraham Ibn Ezra, a 12th-century rabbi, with discovering that Moses did not write all of the Pentateuch (the first five books of the Old Testament). Ezra, wrote Spinoza, "confined himself to dark hints which I shall not scruple to elucidate, thus throwing full light on the subject." Spinoza's "light" consisted of denying the Mosaic authorship altogether: "it is thus clearer than the sun at noonday that the Pentateuch was not written by Moses, but by someone who lived long after Moses."[22]

Spinoza was not the first writer of his century to question the Mosaic authorship of the Pentateuch. In *Leviathan* (1651), Thomas Hobbes (another notorious heretic) conceded that Moses may have written much of the Pentateuch, but he also argued that Moses "did not compile those books entirely, and in the form that we now have them." But the pioneer of modern biblical criticism was Isaac La Peyrère, a renegade Calvinist who espoused his own peculiar brand of mysticism and messianism. Writing a decade before Hobbes,

La Peyrère altogether denied the Mosaic authorship of the Pentateuch, identified biblical inaccuracies and contradictions, proclaimed the existence of mankind before Adam, denied the universality of the flood, and embraced many other heretical views. (La Peyrère later abjured—insincerely, under threat of force—over 100 such heresies.) Spinoza was familiar with La Peyrère's ideas and incorporated many of them in his *Treatise*.

Authorship of the Pentateuch may strike the modern reader as an esoteric controversy, a topic scarcely important enough to become excited or upset about, and certainly nothing that would warrant punishing anyone who denies that Moses wrote the first five books of the Bible. But this attitude, which seems commonsensical to many people today, merely illustrates how drastically things have changed over the past several centuries. In Spinoza's day to deny the Mosaic authorship was widely regarded as a dangerous heresy, one punishable by law, because it called into question the status of the Bible as a divinely inspired document. Both orthodox Christians and their critics understood that the authenticity of a purported revelation depends on the credentials of its human messenger, or "prophet." A miracle, if reported by a divinely inspired prophet, was deemed authentic; but that same miracle degenerated into a tall yarn if reported by an unknown and uninspired storyteller. As the deist Thomas Paine explained in *The Age of Reason*,

> Take away from Genesis the belief that Moses was the author, on which only the strange belief that it is the word of God has stood, and there remains nothing of *Genesis*, but an anonymous book of stories, fables, and traditionary or invented absurdities, or downright lies.

In the *Treatise*, Spinoza attempted to render the Bible useless as a source of knowledge—at least for those who are able to reason philosophically. Biblical narratives, he argued, may sometimes illustrate moral precepts, such as justice and charity, but unaided reason can discover those virtues as well, without recourse to revelation (and with more certainty). So of what use is the Bible? Spinoza replied that most people lack the inclination or ability to follow a long chain of philosophic reasoning, so they must learn their morality from easily digested stories and examples. That is where the Bible plays an important role. It does not provide definitions or proof, so it cannot provide the knowledge available through reason; but the Bible's "sayings and reasonings are adapted to the understanding of the masses." Belief in the Bible (or certain parts of it) "is particularly necessary to the masses whose intellect is not capable of perceiving things clearly and distinctly." In addition, ordinary people are likely to read biblical stories without grasping their moral import, so the masses "are always in need of pastors or church ministers to explain them to their feeble intelligence."

Spinoza's derogatory remarks about the "masses" exhibited an intellectual and moral elitism that would run throughout the history of freethought well into the 18th-century Enlightenment. Voltaire, for example, regarded Christian doctrines as unworthy of enlightened minds, while insisting that those selfsame doctrines were necessary to keep the unenlightened masses from running amok, morally speaking. But not all freethinkers shared this attitude. Many 18th-century freethinkers—such as the deists Peter Annet, Thomas Chubb, and Thomas Paine—specifically tailored their anti-Christian tracts for the common man, believing that the average person is capable of thinking for himself and arriving at rational judgments; and that attitude became dominant among 19th-century freethinkers. Government authorities typically regarded the "vulgar" popularization of freethought as a greater threat to the religious and political status quo than the more sophisticated treatments intended for academics and intellectuals. Nevertheless, when modern historians discuss the history of freethought, they almost always focus on the academic freethinkers; they typically dismiss those I call the "street freethinkers"—who wrote in a style that would appeal to the masses—as unworthy of serious consideration.

For Spinoza, as for many deists, the essence of a good religion is its ability to improve moral conduct. A person may believe every word of the Bible, but if that belief does not make him more virtuous, "he might employ himself just as profitably in reading the Koran or the poetic drama, or ordinary chronicles." In contrast, a person may be wholly ignorant of the Bible or deny its divine status, but if he is a good person who leads a moral life, then "he is absolutely blessed and truly possesses in himself the spirit of Christ." The natural light of reason, for those skilled in its use, is sufficient to show us "the true way of salvation."

With this background, we can understand why the *Theologico-Political Treatise* generated a maelstrom among Spinoza's contemporaries and for many decades thereafter. Few books have been so universally reviled. Although some theologians—Catholic, Protestant, and Jewish—invested reason with an important and independent role, they still insisted that revelation provides knowledge inaccessible and superior to reason, knowledge essential to salvation. Spinoza would have none of this. Reason, he insisted, is supreme and sufficient. If people "hawk about something superior to reason, it is mere figment, and far below reason." Spinoza was "thoroughly convinced, that the Bible leaves reason absolutely free, that it has nothing in common with philosophy, in fact, that Revelation and Philosophy stand on totally different footings. . . . Each has its separate province, neither can be called the handmaid of the other."

That statement sounds like an important concession to revelation; but, as we have seen, the "province" that Spinoza assigned to revelation is rather mundane. Obedience, not knowledge, is the "sole object" of revelation, and even then revelation is needed only when dealing with the dull-witted masses. The Bible does not presume to teach philosophy or science "but only very simple matters, such as could be understood by the slowest intelligence."

Do reason and revelation conflict? Early in the *Treatise*, Spinoza remarked that he found nothing "taught expressly by Scripture, which does not agree with our understanding, or which is repugnant thereto." This apparent concession was a bit misleading, however. Later in the *Treatise*, Spinoza stated, "I insist that [the Bible] expressly affirms and teaches that God is jealous . . . and I assert that such a doctrine is repugnant to reason." After mentioning additional irrational teachings, Spinoza pushed his case even further. He asserted that the Bible contains many contradictions, thereby exposing the "absurdities" of accepting the Bible as a source of knowledge.

How do we reconcile Spinoza's claim that the Bible and reason are consistent with his laundry list of biblical absurdities and contradictions? Quite simply: reason gives us knowledge whereas revelation does not. Reason conflicts with revelation only if we take the Bible to be something more than a collection of moral lessons directed to those who cannot "acquire the habit of virtue under the unaided guide of reason." The Bible is useful but not necessarily true. Reason reigns supreme in all matters of knowledge; it is "the light of the mind, and without her all things are dreams and phantoms."

Perhaps the most scandalous part of the *Theologico-Political Treatise* was its unequivocal rejection of miracles. A miracle is said to be an event that contravenes the laws of nature. According to Spinoza, however, those natural laws are themselves manifestations of the divine nature. To say that God contravened natural law is to say that God "acted against his own nature—an evident absurdity." Indeed, since we perceive God through the "immutable order of nature," our knowledge of God increases along with our understanding of nature. But a miracle defies rational comprehension, so it actually diminishes our knowledge of God.

In addition, a miracle would be an insult to the divine nature: it implies that "God has created nature so weak, and has ordained for her laws so barren," that he must repeatedly tinker with his flawed creation through miracles. Deists would later have a field day with this argument. It was even used by the German philosopher Gottfried Wilhelm Leibniz against the claim of Isaac Newton that God must occasionally intervene in the natural course of events to keep the universe running properly. That line of thinking would suggest, according to Leibniz (who was not a religious skeptic), that an omnipotent and omniscient deity was unable to create a perfect universe on the first try.

15

Spinoza on Freedom of Religion and Speech

From a libertarian perspective, there is good news and bad news about the political theory of Benedict Spinoza. The good news, which I discuss in this chapter, is his magnificent defense of freedom of religion and speech, and how he based his defense on a theory of inalienable rights. The bad news, which I discuss in the next chapter, is Spinoza's quasi-Hobbesian theory of rights and government in which the right to do x means nothing more than the power, or ability, to do x. The sovereign, for Spinoza as for Hobbes, has the right to do whatever he has the power to do. The sovereign's obligation to respect the liberty of his subjects is solely a matter of self-interest; the mistreatment of subjects is bound to generate resentment and possibly seditious tendencies, and those sentiments, in turn, will render the sovereign's authority less secure than it would otherwise be. Moreover, despite his apparent defense of absolute freedom of speech, Spinoza specified certain exceptions that are bound to annoy modern libertarians. But, as I said, I will relate the details of the bad news in the next chapter. Here, I turn to the good news.

Defenses of religious toleration had been published before Spinoza entered the fray in 1670 with his *Theologico-Political Treatise*, but his treatment stands out in at least two respects. First, Spinoza reduced authentic religion to overt conduct—specifically, acts of justice and charity—and he regarded the beliefs and motives that prompt such conduct as irrelevant to political society. As long as you respect the rights of others, *why* you do so doesn't matter. The state should concern itself only with external actions and should have no concern with your beliefs, whether rational or irrational, moral or immoral, orthodox or heretical. Thus, Spinoza admitted no exceptions to his principle of religious freedom. Unlike many earlier defenders of toleration, he did not exclude atheists, Jews, Catholics, and the like.

Second, Spinoza grounded freedom of religion in the broader principle of freedom of speech. Every person, whether or not religious, has the inalienable right to express his beliefs (with some exceptions, to be discussed later). He wrote,

> The most tyrannical governments are those which make crimes of opinions, for everyone has an inalienable right over his thoughts—nay, such a state of things leads to the rule of popular passion. . . . To avoid such evils in a state, there is no safer way than to make piety and religion to consist in acts only— that is, in the practice of justice and charity, leaving everyone's judgments in other respects free.

Spinoza's mention of inalienable rights is highly significant; indeed, this concept is the foundation of his argument for freedom of conscience. For Spinoza as for classical liberals generally, an inalienable right is a right that is inextricably linked to man's reason and moral agency. Thus, since we literally cannot transfer our power of judgment and choice to another person, including a sovereign, we cannot transfer or otherwise abdicate our inalienable rights, even if we wish to do so. Even a slave must decide whether to obey his master or suffer the consequences; this power of decision-making is inherent in human nature and inseparable from it. The political upshot of this theory is that, since inalienable rights can never be transferred, even with the agent's consent, no sovereign can rightfully claim dominion over those rights. (See my discussion of inalienable rights in "The Philosophy of the Declaration of Independence, Part 2."[23]) Spinoza put it this way:

> No man's mind can possibly lie wholly at the disposition of another, for no one can willingly transfer his natural right of free reason and judgment, or be compelled so to do. For this reason government which attempts to control minds is accounted tyrannical, and it is considered an abuse of sovereignty and a usurpation of the rights of subjects, to seek to prescribe what shall be accepted as true, or rejected as false, or what opinions should actuate men in their worship of God. All these questions fall within a man's natural right, which he cannot abdicate even with his own consent.

When a sovereign attempts to control the beliefs of his subjects, he attempts, in effect, to do what cannot possibly be done, something that lies outside his power. When a person transfers certain rights to a sovereign with the hope of establishing a just system of law, he "justly cedes the right of free action, though not of free reason." From that premise, Spinoza moved, somewhat tenuously, to the right of free speech. It is virtually impossible for people to keep silent about their core beliefs. "Since, therefore, no one can abdicate his freedom of judgment and feeling; since every man is by indefeasible natural right the master of his own thoughts, it follows that men thinking in diverse and contradictory fashions, cannot, without disastrous results, be compelled to speak only according to the dictates of the supreme power."

Of course, Spinoza understood that "freedom may be crushed" to the point that people "do not dare to utter a whisper, save at the bidding of their ruler." But even that degree of tyranny cannot prevent people from thinking for themselves. So what will happen if a ruler exercises such power? Simply this: "men [will] daily be thinking one thing and saying another"—a practice that will weave deceit and hypocrisy into the social fabric, thereby permitting "the avaricious, the flatterers, and other numskulls" to rise to the top. The truly creative and worthwhile members in such a society will not subordinate their opinions to the arbitrary decrees of a tyrant; they will become martyrs to freedom and "raise feelings of pity and revenge" in the general population, after which plots to overthrow the tyrant will surely emerge. As a ruler becomes more tyrannical, his hold on power will become less secure. In the final analysis, a ruler with "sound judgment" will not attempt to extend his power beyond reasonable limits. A ruler who limits his power to external behavior while leaving thoughts and speech unmolested will find little to fear from seditious plots.

> Such seditions only spring up, when law enters the domain of speculative thought, and opinions are put on trial and condemned on the same footing as crimes, while those who defend and follow them are sacrificed, not to public safety, but to their opponents' hatred and cruelty. If deeds only could be made the grounds of criminal charges, and words were always allowed to pass free, such seditions would be divested of every semblance of justification, and would be separated from mere controversies by a hard and fast line.

But consider the common argument that freedom of belief and speech may sometimes result in pernicious social consequences. What then? Spinoza did not deny the possibility; he simply considered it irrelevant, pointing out that the beneficial consequences of freedom far outweigh its potential harm. He also claimed that any attempt to suppress personal vices is likely to make those vices worse, not better.

> We cannot doubt that the best government will allow freedom of philosophical speculation no less than of religious belief. I confess that from such freedom

inconveniences may sometimes arise, but what question was ever settled so wisely that no abuses could possibly spring therefrom? He who seeks to regulate everything by law, is more likely to arouse vices than to reform them. It is best to grant what cannot be abolished, even though it be in itself harmful. How many evils spring from luxury, envy, avarice, drunkenness, and the like, yet these are tolerated—vices as they are—because they cannot be prevented by legal enactments. How much more then should free thought be granted, seeing that it is in itself a virtue and that it cannot be crushed! . . . Such freedom is absolutely necessary for progress in science and the liberal arts; for no man follows such pursuits to advantage unless his judgment be entirely free and unhampered.

Holland in Spinoza's day was famous for its high degree of religious freedom, and he was understandably proud of his native country. Near the beginning of his *Treatise*, Spinoza recommended the Dutch model as an example that would eliminate much of the religious discord and strife found in other countries:

Now, seeing that we have the rare happiness of living in a republic, where everyone's judgment is free and unshackled, where each may worship God as his conscience dictates, and where freedom is esteemed before all things dear and precious, I have believed that I should be undertaking no ungrateful or unprofitable task, in demonstrating that not only can such freedom be granted without prejudice to the public peace, but also, that without such freedom, piety cannot flourish nor the public peace be secure.

Much later in the *Treatise*, Spinoza discussed Amsterdam and the many benefits, including economic benefits, that had accrued from its respect for the religious freedom of everyone:

The city of Amsterdam reaps the fruit of this [religious] freedom in its own great prosperity and in the admiration of all other people. For in this most flourishing state, and most splendid city, men of every nation and religion live together in the greatest harmony, and ask no questions before trusting their goods to a fellow-citizen, save whether he be rich or poor, and whether he generally acts honestly, or the reverse. His religion and sect is considered of no importance: for it has no effect before the judges in gaining or losing a cause, and there is no sect so despised that its followers, provided that they harm no one, pay every man his due, and live uprightly, are deprived of the protection of the magisterial authority.

Spinoza was not the only writer to note the connection between religious freedom and commercial prosperity. Voltaire made a similar observation as a result of the years he spent in England. In *Philosophical Letters* (1733), Voltaire pointed out how commercial freedom and the self-interested desire for profit tend to trump religious prejudice:

> Enter the London stock exchange, that place more respectable than many a court. You will see the deputies of all nations gathered there for the service of mankind. There the Jew, the Mohammedan, and the Christian deal with each other as if they were of the same religion, and give the name of infidel only to those who go bankrupt; there the Presbyterian trusts the Anabaptist, and the Anglican accepts the Quaker's promise. On leaving these peaceful and free assemblies, some go to the synagogue, others go to drink; this one goes to have himself baptized in the name of the Father, through the Son, to the Holy Ghost; that one has his son's foreskin cut off and Hebrew words mumbled over the child which he does

not understand; others go to their church to await the inspiration of God, their hats on their heads, and all are content.

On several occasions in previous chapters, I have called attention to the fundamental role that freedom of conscience played in the evolution of classical liberalism. That focus is brilliantly illustrated in the writings of Spinoza, the much maligned "atheist." Part of this emphasis obviously grew from the ferocious and bloody religious conflicts that plagued post-Reformation Europe. But more was involved. Theoretically speaking, freedom of conscience was the sun around which other freedoms, including economic freedom, revolved. As classical liberals saw the matter, freedom of conscience extends far beyond religion. Without freedom of conscience no other freedoms are possible.

16

Spinoza's Political Theory

Benedict Spinoza presented his political theory in two works: the *Theologico-Political Treatise* (beginning with chapter 16), published anonymously in 1670; and *A Political Treatise*, an unfinished book that was published posthumously in 1677, the year of Spinoza's death. Although the latter book presents one of the earliest defenses of democracy ever written, its discussion of Spinoza's fundamental ideas about rights and sovereignty does little more than summarize the more extensive treatment found in the former.

In an age when it was increasingly common to write scholarly books in the vernacular, Spinoza wrote everything in Latin, and he did so for what he regarded as a compelling reason. As he explained in the preface to the *Theological-Political Treatise*, only educated philosophical readers were likely to give his ideas a fair hearing: "To the rest of mankind I care not to commend my treatise, for I cannot expect that it contains anything to please them." Most educated readers in Spinoza's day could read Latin, which had served for centuries as the universal language among Europeans (as French would later do, and as English does now). Most of the common people could not read Latin; and Spinoza viewed the "multitude" as so filled with "prejudices embraced under the name of religion" and so prone "to praise or blame by impulse rather than by reason" that it was better for them not to read the *Treatise* at all rather than "misinterpret it after their wont." Utter neglect by the masses was preferable to the outcry that his ideas—especially his call for freedom of religion and his denial that "Reason is a mere handmaid to Theology"—might provoke among the common people if those ideas became widely known. Such an outcry might jeopardize Spinoza's personal safety and lead to the censorship of his writings (a measure advocated by many of his critics, even in liberal Holland), in which case the *Treatise* might become unavailable to those who stood to benefit from it the most.

Spinoza concluded the preface with a type of political gen-
uflection that was regarded as a necessary safety measure
by many freethinkers of his time. "I have written nothing,"
he declared, "which I do not most willingly submit to the
examination and judgment of my country's rulers, and that
I am ready to retract anything, which they shall decide to
be repugnant to the laws or prejudicial to the public good."
Spinoza had "taken scrupulous care, and striven to keep in
entire accordance with the laws of my country, with loyalty,
and with morality."

Spinoza's controversial ideas extended beyond the realm of
religion into the realm of politics, both theoretical and practical. In Spinoza's political ideas lurk the ghosts of Niccolò
Machiavelli and Thomas Hobbes: a defense of "realpolitik"
that claimed to base politics on the stark realities of human
nature, on man as he really *is* rather than man as we think
he *ought* to be. This perspective led Spinoza to repudiate the
conventional *moral* nature of rights and to substitute a purely
descriptive account of rights that equated rights with sheer
power. According to Spinoza, what we have the *power* to do
we also have the *right* to do. Spinoza, a strict determinist,
believed that human nature impels every individual to seek
his own preservation and welfare, so we have a right to take

whatever measures we deem necessary to achieve those ends, however incorrect or irrational our judgments may be. As he put it in the *Treatise*,

> Whatsoever, therefore, an individual (considered as under the sway of nature) thinks useful for himself, whether led by sound reason or impelled by the passions, that he has a sovereign right to seek and to take for himself as he best can, whether by force, cunning, entreaty, or any other means; consequently he may regard as an enemy anyone who hinders the accomplishment of his purpose.

Spinoza applied his purely naturalistic conception of a "right" to all living entities, not merely to human beings. Thus, large fish have the sovereign right to devour small fish because such behavior is inherent in their natures. Spinoza reached this conclusion by personifying nature, as when he wrote that "it is certain that Nature, taken in the abstract, has sovereign right to do anything she can; in other words, her right is co-extensive with her power." Hence, the rights of human beings are limited only by their powers. This principle applies as much to *irrational* actions and persons as it does to *rational* actions and persons. Spinoza, of course, was a great champion of reason and defended its indispensable role in the pursuit of happiness. But he also understood that most people are motivated largely by their passions, however destructive to oneself and others those passions may be. Passions that generate irrational behavior are part of human nature, so rights do not vary according to the rationality of the acting agent. Just as "the wise man has sovereign right . . . to live according to the laws of reason, so also the ignorant and foolish man has sovereign right to . . . live according to the laws of desire." Expecting a foolish, irrational man to live like a thoughtful, rational man is like expecting a cat to live according to "the laws of the nature of a lion."

Spinoza rejected the notion of a universe that is intrinsically rational. Nature, per se, is neither rational nor irrational; to render any such judgment is to impose on nature a human judgment. Man is a mere "speck" in the cosmos, a being whose first and primary natural impulse is to preserve his own being. If some methods of survival strike us as better or more rational than other methods, this is true only from our limited perspective: "nature is not bounded by the laws of human reason, which aims only at man's true benefit and preservation." If some human actions appear to us evil, immoral, or unjust, this is only because we are ignorant of the ways of nature in the broadest sense; "in reality that which reason considers evil, is not evil in respect to the order and laws of nature as a whole, but only in respect to the laws of our reason." These and similar comments are closely related to Spinoza's insistence that philosophers should study human passions objectively, as entomologists study bugs. The goal of a philosopher is to understand how our passions influence our actions, not to assess those passions as good or bad, right or wrong, rational or irrational.

Thus, Spinoza asserted that power and right are coextensive, that we have a right to do anything we regard as useful to our own preservation and welfare. From there, it follows that people in a state of nature (a society without government) are "natural enemies." If I deem it useful to kill you so that I can expropriate your property, then I have the "right" to kill you. And from that unlimited right, perpetual social conflict will inevitably ensue. This premise is thoroughly Hobbesian, despite the considerable efforts of philosophers sympathetic to Spinoza to distance him from the odious Hobbes. That is not to say Spinoza agreed with Hobbes down the line. There were significant differences between the two, most notably Spinoza's repudiation of political absolutism in favor of democracy, his defense of freedom of speech and religion, and so forth. Indeed, in contrast to Hobbes, Spinoza made it clear that individual freedom should be the ultimate goal of government:

> The object of government is not to change men from rational beings into beasts or puppets, but to enable them to develop their minds and bodies in security, and to employ their reason unshackled; neither showing hatred, anger, or deceit, nor watched with the eyes of jealousy and injustice. In fact, the true aim of government is liberty.

So, how did Spinoza get from his Hobbesian premises (such as the claim that justice and injustice do not exist in a state of nature but are determined solely by government) to his defense of an essentially free society? The journey was a bumpy ride, to say the least. Spinoza maintained that people will come to understand that their interests are best served by leaving the state of nature, an anarchistic condition where people may do anything they have the power to do, and by agreeing to form a civil society; in civil society, they transfer their right of free action in favor of a government that will determine which actions are just and permissible and which actions are not. This version of the social contract is peculiar, since Spinoza's conception of a "right" has no moral element that would permit us to say that people, whether rulers or the ruled, are *morally* obligated to respect their part of the social contract.

Spinoza did not flinch when considering this problem; rather, he held doggedly to his naturalistic conception of rights while defending his version of social contract theory. Consider a democracy, a civil society in which the people as a whole control government. The right of the people to rule is based on nothing more than the majority possessing greater power than the minority, which enables the majority to enforce its common will against dissenters. And it is precisely this greater power that gives them the right to rule. The government in a democracy, which supposedly speaks for the people, can pass any laws it likes and is *able to enforce*. As we would expect in Spinoza's theory, the rights of a government are identical to its power. Whatever a government *can* do, it has the *right* to do by virtue of its superior power to enforce its will.

So where can individual freedom possibly find refuge in Spinoza's thoroughly anti-libertarian theory of rights? I covered Spinoza's answer in the previous chapter, explaining his theory of *inalienable* rights. To reiterate, inalienable rights, according to Spinoza, are those rights (i.e., powers) that are so embedded in human nature that they cannot possibly be transferred, abandoned, or otherwise alienated in *any* circumstances. It is therefore absurd, because it is impossible, for any government to claim dominion over such rights. Governmental power is limited by human nature itself, not by moral principles based on reason. Since no government can do what cannot possibly be done, since no government has the power to accomplish the impossible, no government can claim the right to control freedom of speech and religion and other rights based on the inalienable powers of human beings.

In addition (and also discussed in the preceding chapter), a democratic government must retain the respect of the people if it wishes to elicit obedience to its laws and decrees. People will regard a government as desirable only if they believe that life under that government is preferable to a state of nature or to another government; current rulers will be able to retain their power only as long as they do not lapse into tyranny. And, in line with Spinoza's theory of rights, a government that loses its *ability* to rule also loses its *right* to rule.

Spinoza's theory of rights and government may strike libertarian readers as downright bizarre. Welcome to the club. I regard it as a massive failure, considered as a whole, and an embarrassing failure to boot. How someone with Spinoza's brilliance and passionate love of freedom could defend such a rickety theory remains a mystery to me. Its holes are so huge and obvious that I hesitate to point them out, for fear of insulting the intelligence of my readers. Nevertheless, I will run that risk in the next chapter, where I discuss some objections to Spinoza's political theory in particular and to the realpolitik approach in general. Philosophers who pride themselves on their political realism, and who repudiate and ridicule the supposedly soft-headed, speculative reasoning of those philosophers who defend the conventional notion (in classical liberalism) of natural rights, often end up producing the most god-awful philosophical mush imaginable.

17

A Critique of Spinoza

In a previous chapter, I explained Benedict Spinoza's defense of freedom of speech and religion. These principles, along with his defense of democracy, might seem to make Spinoza an important figure in the early history of classical liberalism. And so he was, but only to a very limited extent. As I explained in the previous chapter, Spinoza defended the Hobbesian position that we have the *right* to do whatever we have the *power* to do. In thus rendering rights coextensive with power, Spinoza insisted that men are "natural enemies" who, while pursuing their self-preservation and welfare in a state of nature without government, would have the unlimited right to take any actions they deem conducive to those ends, including acts of violence against innocents who had not harmed them in any manner.

Spinoza refused to call invasive acts committed in a state of nature "unjust." The concepts of just and unjust actions arise only under the jurisdiction of a sovereign government. In *A Political Treatise*, for example, Spinoza wrote that justice and injustice "in their strict sense . . . cannot be conceived of, except under [political] dominion. For nature offers nothing that can be called this man's rather than another's; but under nature everything belongs to all—that is, they have authority to claim it for themselves." Only with a government that has enacted a legal code and has the power to enforce its laws do these ideas come into play. (This assertion is obviously false, since we can easily conceive of property rights and just and unjust actions in a society without government. Whether we believe that such rights can adequately be *enforced* in a state of nature is a different issue.)

Even Spinoza's defense of religious freedom, which is fine as far as it goes, is seriously undercut by his refusal to extend freedom to *external* religious practices. According to Spinoza, if we have an inalienable right to *believe* whatever we like, it is because our power to believe or not believe cannot be compelled by physical force or threats of force. Given that a government, like an individual, has the right to do whatever it has the power to do, we cannot properly say that a govern- ment has a right to dictate our religious beliefs because no government can possibly accomplish that goal. But the same is not true of external religious practices, such as sacred rites and ceremonies. The sovereign has the power, and therefore the right, to control such practices, permitting some and forbidding others. Spinoza, like Thomas Hobbes and some other critics of institutionalized religion, defended a position known as Erastianism (after the Swiss theologian Thomas Erastus, 1524–1583), according to which churches and religious practices generally should be under the absolute control of the sovereign secular state.

Much of Spinoza's concern with religious practices lay in his understanding of the power that religion has to motivate human action, especially when a state issues decrees that are widely viewed as contrary to divine law. Churches, most notably the Catholic Church, had often served as a buffer, or intermediate power, between the individual and the state and had thereby prevented the state from exercising its (supposedly) legitimate authority. (That is why Hobbes, who agreed with Spinoza that a sovereign should not attempt to dictate the *personal* religious beliefs of citizens but should control *external* religious practices, likened the Catholic Church to "worms in the entrails of a natural man.") Churches, moreover, were frequently behind political resistance, rebellions, and revolutions, so Spinoza demanded that all such institutions be kept under the thumb of the state to prevent such calamities. Since the primary function of government is to maintain peace and social order, anything that promotes seditious tendencies should not be allowed to roam free. The restriction applies not only to institutions but also to seditious books and speech, which Spinoza specified as exceptions to his general presumption of freedom. Thus, although Spinoza did not wish churches to wield any political power, he did not defend the separation of church and state, as we now understand that expression. Rather, he argued that churches should be subservient to the state, and that religious believers should obey all state demands regarding rites and ceremonies, however personally offensive they may be.

Thus, we see how Spinoza was a mixed bag from a libertarian perspective. True, he believed that a sovereign should be rational, which means that a sovereign should impose only those restrictions on freedom necessary to maintain peace and social order, creating a society in which individuals can pursue their own interests without coercive interference. However, Spinoza also believed that the vast majority of people are irrational, that they are guided by their passions instead of by their reason—this, after all, is why they need a government to restrain their actions; but he had no grounds for defending the superior rationality of rulers, who are as likely as anyone else to succumb to their lusts and other irrational desires. The only restraint on a ruler is his own preservation and welfare, so a rational ruler will not push oppressive laws to the point where citizens become so outraged that they attempt to overthrow him. But in Spinoza's scheme, there is no *moral* principle of individual rights that would render *anything* a ruler attempts to do *unjust* in the libertarian understanding of that term. For Spinoza, therefore, there is no right to resist (or even to disobey) oppressive laws, much less a right to overthrow tyrannical governments. As he put it, "however iniquitous the subject may think the commonwealth's decisions, he is none the less bound to execute them." The rights of an organized political society, where the sovereign represents the collective will of the people, are rooted solely in the fact that the many are more powerful than the individual. As Spinoza put it, "the body and mind of a dominion have as much right as they have power. And thus each single citizen or subject has the less right, the more the commonwealth exceeds him in power."

Let us now consider some brief objections to Spinoza's political theory. First, as noted previously, Spinoza repeatedly observed that most people are governed by their passions, not by their reason; yet he also argued that in an ideal government rulers self-limit their powers according to rational calculations of utility. Rational rulers understand that tyrannical measures will ultimately diminish their power and are therefore detrimental to their own self-interest. But why should we assume that rulers are, or will be, more rational than the many irrational people they rule? If history proves anything, it proves the exact opposite. Many rulers throughout history would have been leading candidates for the first available vacancy in a lunatic asylum. Spinoza's rational rulers smack of Plato's philosopher-kings; both ideas are dangerously naïve.

Second, Spinoza used his theory of inalienable rights to argue that no ruler may claim dominion over freedom of religion and speech. But even if we agree that no ruler can possibly control those practices in every detail, it does not follow that rulers lack the power to *make the attempt.* The ability to achieve a goal and the ability to *try* to achieve that selfsame goal are two different things. Countless rulers have attempted to control the religion and speech of their subjects; however much they may have failed, they obviously had the power to make the effort and *believed* they would attain the desired ends. At the very least, therefore, if we follow Spinoza's identification of rights with power, we need to say that rulers have the *right* (since they have the power) to *attempt* to suppress freedom of religion and speech. Spinoza did not wish to end up at that point, but it does follow logically from his theory of rights.

Third, the problems I have mentioned so far pale in comparison with the problems attending any attempt to identify rights with powers. Yes, we may have the *power* to murder other people or to enslave them, but in what sense may this power be said to confer a *right* to murder and enslave? There is serious ambiguity in any such assertion, which haunts Spinoza's entire discussion. Did Spinoza mean to say that our power to do *x* confers on us the right to do *x* in a *moral* sense? If so, then our right must entail a *duty* by others to respect our right to do *x*. But I highly doubt that is what Spinoza intended to say; he expressly affirmed that the distinction between just and unjust actions depends entirely on the decrees of a government and would not exist in a state of nature. Rather, Spinoza appears to mean that there is *no difference* between power and right, that they are one and the same concept. But if that is the case, then to derive rights from power is a useless and misleading redundancy. If whenever we say "I have the right to do *x*," we simply mean "I have the power to do *x*," then the term "right" adds no new information. It simply repeats what was said before, with no change in meaning.

Many classical liberals criticized the effort to identify power with rights. (Whether they were criticizing Hobbes or Spinoza, or both, is not always clear.) One of the best comments is found in William Wollaston's important book,

The Religion of Nature Delineated. First published in the early 1720s and running through eight editions, the book was a bestseller in its day that attracted the attention of many better-known philosophers, including David Hume, Thomas Jefferson, and Jeremy Bentham. In considering the proposition that we have the right to do whatever we have the power to do, Wollaston wrote, "*power* and *right,* or a power of doing any thing, and right to do it, are quite different ideas: and therefore they may be separated, nor does one infer the other." Wollaston continued,

> If *power, qua* power, gives a right to dominion, it gives a right to *every thing*, that is obnoxious to it; and then nothing can be done that is wrong. (For no body can do any thing which he has not the *power* to do.) [This] is to advance a plain *absurdity* or *contradiction* rather. For then to oppose the man who has this *power*, as far as one can, or (which is the same) as far as one has the *power* to do it, would not be wrong: yet so it must be, if he has a right to dominion, or not to be opposed.

Understanding Wollaston's point is crucial here. It may be restated as follows: If we equate "rights" with "power," then it is literally *impossible* to violate anyone's rights, since we cannot do anything that we lack the power to do. Suppose someone assaults you in an effort to steal your money. He has the right to make this assault, according to Spinoza, because he has the power, or ability, to attack you. But you likewise have the right to resist his assault if you have the power to resist. And he, in turn, has the right to counteract your defense if he is able, while you, in turn, have the right (if you have the power) to fight on. And so on indefinitely, until we are lost in a tumultuous sea of conflicting rights.

As traditionally conceived—not only in classical liberalism but in other political traditions as well—rights were the flip side of moral obligations. Thus, if you have a right to x, I have the obligation not to coercively interfere with your use and disposal of x. Rights were regarded as principles that distinguish between *mine* and *thine* in a social context. To equate rights with power makes mincemeat of this important distinction and ultimately reduces to redundancy or nonsense. In the final analysis, Spinoza's theory of rights amounts to saying nothing more than that we have the power to do whatever we have the power to do.

18

Jean Meslier

Jean Meslier (1664–1729) was an obscure and—by all accounts—kindly French priest who would not be remembered today if not for a manuscript he left behind for his parishioners. Commonly known as *The Testament of Jean Meslier*, this lengthy book (97 chapters and more than 550 pages in the recent English translation) is an outright and highly polemical defense of atheism.[24] Although the complete French manuscript was not published until 1864, Meslier's *Testament* exerted a profound influence on French freethinkers during the 18th century, especially Denis Diderot and Baron d'Holbach. (A more accurate and critical edition came in 2007, followed by the first complete English translation ever in 2009.) Meslier reportedly made three copies of his manuscript; in subsequent decades, as other copies were made and circulated, the *Testament* became a highly prized item in the French underground, or clandestine, book market. After Voltaire obtained a copy, he praised Meslier as a "good priest" and recommended that his book be a constant companion of educated readers. But when Voltaire published his highly abridged extract from the *Testament*, he added material that made Meslier seem a deist (like Voltaire himself) rather than the atheist he really was.

I first became familiar with Meslier's *Testament*—or thought I did—while in high school during the 1960s, when I read a book titled *Superstition in All Ages*, published by the American freethought publisher Peter Eckler. Although this book represents itself as a condensed, translated version of Meslier's *Testament*, it is nothing of the sort. It is in fact a translation of a book, *Good Sense*, by d'Holbach—a German atheist—and may be called a condensed version of d'Holbach's much more extensive two-volume work, *The System of Nature* (originally published in 1770 under the pseudonym "Mirabaud"). I have never been able to determine with certitude how far back this conflation of texts goes, but it may have started in the 18th century.

The French philosopher and historian of atheism Michel Onfray said this of Meslier's *Testament*:

> For the first time (but how long will it take us to acknowledge this?) in the history of ideas, a

philosopher had dedicated a whole book to the question of atheism. He professed it, demonstrated it, arguing and quoting, sharing his reading and his reflections, and seeking confirmation from his own observations of the everyday world. His title sets it out clearly: *Memoir of the Thoughts and Feelings of Jean Meslier*; and so does his subtitle: *Clear and Evident Demonstrations of the Vanity and Falsity of All the Religions of the World*. The book appeared in 1729, after his death. Meslier had spent the greater part of his life working on it. The history of true atheism had begun.[25]

I think it is an exaggeration to say that the "history of true atheism" began with Meslier. Even a quick perusal of the richly documented study by Alan Charles Kors, *Atheism in France: 1650–1729* (Princeton, 1990) should dispel that notion. But the historical significance of the *Testament* cannot be denied. Its significance goes far beyond its unremitting attacks on Christianity (including the Bible) and supernaturalistic religions generally. The *Testament* is also important for its strident libertarianism. Although I would not go so far as Onfray does in dubbing Meslier an "anarchist" (various remarks by Meslier seem to conflict with this characterization), his hatred of governmental oppression, expressed in clear, forceful, and unequivocal language, was highly unusual in his day.

Since the *Testament* is unknown to the vast majority of modern libertarians, I devote this and the next several chapters to explaining its ideas. This chapter focuses on Meslier's libertarianism. (Exactly what kind of libertarian was Meslier? I discuss that issue in chapter 21.) I provide generous quotations from the *Testament* in the hope that they will motivate fellow libertarians to read the book for themselves.

An especially interesting feature of Meslier's thinking about government is his reliance on the libertarian classic *Discourse on Voluntary Servitude* by Étienne de La Boétie (1530–1563). Like La Boétie, Meslier insisted that rulers could not maintain their power without the tacit cooperation of the people they ruled. If that cooperation were denied, political power and oppression would dissolve of their own accord. The following passage from the *Testament* is typical. In considering the issue of why so many of the common people of France were desperately poor, Meslier wrote,

> It is because you and all your fellow men are loaded with all the burdens of the state. You are loaded not only with the burdens of your kings and princes who are your tyrants, but also the burdens of the nobility

and clergy, all the monasticism and the courts, all the lackeys and grooms of the rulers and all the servants of others, all the soldiers, the cellar-rat tax collectors, police of salt and tobacco, and, finally, all the lazy and useless people in the world.

For, it is only from the fruit of your hard work that all these people live. By your work you supply everything necessary for their subsistence and not only what is necessary, but also what they can use for their entertainment and pleasures. What would happen, for example, to the greatest princes and potentates of the earth if the people did not support them? It is only from the people (whom they care so little about) that they get all their grandeur, riches, and power. In a word, they would be nothing but weak, little men like you if you did not support their grandeur. They would not have more riches than you if you did not give them yours. And they would not have more power or authority than you if you did not want to submit to their laws and will.

Another noteworthy aspect of the *Testament* is found in Meslier's argument for legalizing divorce. (He also

thought priests and monks should be allowed to marry.)
Meslier wrote,

> Likewise, if all men, and particularly our Christ cult-
> ists, did not hold marriages indissoluble as they do,
> and if, on the contrary, they always left their unions
> and conjugal relationships free among themselves,
> without forcing each other, i.e., either the men or the
> women, to remain inseparably together all their lives
> against their inclinations, we would certainly not see
> as many bad marriages and households as there are,
> and there would not be as much discord and dissen-
> sion as there is between husbands and wives.

Taxes topped Meslier's list of oppressive government measures. He especially detested tax collectors—"cellar-rats," he
called them—who increased "the harshness of such a hateful and detestable yoke." Innocent, hardworking Frenchmen
were "mistreated every day by a thousand hard and severe
money collectors, who are normally proud and arrogant men
and from whom all people have to suffer all the put-downs,
thefts, fraud, misappropriations, and all kinds of other injus-
tices and mistreatments. For here is no officer, tax collector, or
clerk so petty, no archer officer of salt and tobacco so vile who,

on the pretext of being hired by the king and on the pretext of collecting and hoarding money, does not believe that he has to make them proud and that he has the right to scoff at, mistreat, trample, and tyrannize the poor."

The vast extent of French taxes and commercial regulations also incurred Meslier's wrath:

> On the one hand, these kings levy huge taxes on all kinds of merchandise in order to profit from everything that is bought and sold; they put them on wine and meat; on eau de vie, alcohol, and beer; on wool, linen, and lace; on salt and pepper; on paper, tobacco, and all kinds of commodities. They make them pay for rights of entry and exit; for rights of registration; for marriages, baptisms, and burials, whenever it seems good to them; they make them pay for liquidations, for relief of communities, for the woods and forests and for the rivers. . . . If they see someone doing business on the lands of their dominion and freely coming and going to buy and sell or only to transport merchandise from one place to another, he must have, as is said in the *Apocalypse* [the Book of Revelation], the mark of the beast, i.e., the mark of the tax-collector rats and the permission of the king. He must have

credentials, clearance, passes, passports, receipts, and guarantees and other similar letters of permission that are truly what we can call the mark of the beast, i.e., the mark of the permission of the tyrant. Without this if you are unlucky enough to run into and be seized by the guards or officers of the said royal beast, you run the risk of being ruined and lost because you will be immediately arrested: they will seize, they will confiscate the merchandise, the horses and wagons. In addition to this the merchants or drivers are sentenced to large fines, prison, the galleys, and sometimes even to shameful death, so severely is it forbidden to do business or to come and go with merchandise without having, as I said, the mark of the beast. *And power was given to him . . . that no one could buy or sell except for him who had the mark or name of the beast, or the number of his name* (Rev. 13:17).

Although there were numerous French critics of Louis XIV in early 18th-century France, Meslier's attack was unsurpassed in its vehemence. (Meslier, born in 1664, lived 51 years under the reign of Louis, whose rule spanned over 72 years.) The supposedly great Sun King was in the front rank of those rapacious monarchs who "on a whim" sought to extend the

boundaries of their empires by waging war on their neighbors, using whatever "vain pretexts" they could invent. These
wars of conquest were always undertaken "at the expense of
the lives and goods of the poor," who not only served as can-
non fodder for the French army but who were also forced to
pay for the engine of their own destruction. Moreover, when
armies invade enemy territory, they "ravage and completely
desolate the provinces, burning and bleeding everything."
Meslier wrote of Louis XIV,

> No one has spilled so much blood, killed so many
> men, caused so many tears of widows and orphans,
> ravaged and desolated so many cities and provinces
> as this last, late king Louis XIV, called "the Great"
> truly not for the great and commendable actions he
> did, seeing that he did nothing really worthy of his
> name, but really for the great injustices, the great
> thefts, the great usurpations, the great desolations,
> the great rape and carnage of men that he has caused
> everywhere on land and sea alike.

From a libertarian perspective, one of Meslier's most valuable discussions appears in chapter 58, where he discusses
"the flatterers of kings and princes." (The modern historian

Harry Elmer Barnes, referring to the broader context of rulers in general, expressed the same idea when he criticized those *court* intellectuals and historians who do whatever is needed to justify the policies and actions of their own governments.) Court flatterers, according to Meslier, typically recommend that the sovereign not provide more freedom for his subjects, who will only abuse it. The common people are not wise enough to run their own lives, so the sovereign truly acts for the good of the people by telling them what to do. The people "need to be kept lowly for their own interest."

Court intellectuals do not wish to jeopardize their own positions of power and attendant special privileges. They hope to catch even more financial crumbs as they fall from the sovereign's hands, so they concoct "excessive, empty praise on their behalf." Thus, we see "thousands and thousands of cowardly and villainous flatterers who, in order to get ahead and get more, force themselves to indulge in everything, hiding the flaws and vices of the kings and even turning the vices into virtues or the little talent and virtue they may have [into] a rare and exceptional and even heroic virtue; and they wonderfully exaggerate the little good they happen to do sometimes for some individuals." Magistrates and judges, who are tasked with maintaining impartial justice, "pursue and punish severely the petty criminals; they hang petty thieves and murderers, but they dare to do and say nothing about the great and powerful thieves, the great and powerful murderers and arsonists who devastate the entire earth, who burn and bleed and kill thousands upon thousands of men." (This point is reminiscent of a famous story told about Diogenes, a leading proponent of the Cynic school of moral philosophy in ancient Greece. Observing the arrest of a man who had stolen a bottle, Diogenes quipped, "Lo, the big thieves taking the little one to jail.")

Meslier charged the French clergy with being among the most eager members of the flattering class. Members of the clergy, according to their own religious doctrines, should be "the most zealous defenders of truth and justice and . . . should be the strongest and most faithful protectors of the people against the unjust vexations and attacks of the princes and kings of the earth," but that is not how they actually behaved. Instead, clerics (especially those in higher offices) were often the ones who flattered rulers the most, "and who most cowardly and shamefully betray the duties of their ministry."

Meslier continued with a passage that could have been written by the likes of Thomas Paine, Lysander Spooner, or Murray Rothbard with regard to governments in general:

> Kings and princes are really like ravaging wolves and roaring lions who search for prey; they are always

ready to burden or overburden the people with taxes, always ready to set up new ones and increase the old ones and always ready to ignite the fires of war, and, consequently, always ready to spill blood and take away men's lives.

19

Jean Meslier and the Catholic Church

As I explained in the preceding chapter, the atheist-priest Jean Meslier (1664–1729) indicted both church and state for their roles in oppressing the people of France, especially the poor. He wrote in his *Testament*, "Religion supports the political government as malicious as it may be; and in turn, the political government supports religion as vain and false as it may be." Meslier continued,

> On the one side, the priests, who are the ministers of religion, advise you, under penalty of wrath and eternal damnation, to obey the magistrates, princes, and other sovereigns as being established by God

to govern others; and on the other side, the princes make you respect the priests, they give them good stipends and incomes, they maintain them in the vain and abusive duties of their ministry, they compel the ignorant to look upon as holy and sacred everything they do and everything they order others to do and believe, on the good and specious pretext of religion and the divine cult. And that, once again, is how the errors, abuses, superstitions, impostures, and tyranny were established and how they are maintained to the great misfortune of the poor people who groan under such hard and heavy yokes.

To appreciate Meslier's perspective, we have to understand that in his day the Catholic Church of France did not merely work hand-in-glove with the state; rather, it was an essential *part* of the state, one of the three basic political "estates" of the realm. The "Gallican Church" was more thoroughly integrated with secular authorities than in other Catholic countries. The French king exercised many powers that were normally reserved for the pope, such as the right to assemble church councils and the right to appoint bishops and archbishops. As a consequence of the latter power, almost all the bishops and archbishops in France were noblemen or sons of the king's ministers—men who often had little interest in religion, who lived worldly lives, and who owed allegiance to the king. A bishop need not even reside within the territory of his diocese, and his practical duties were typically performed by canons, an administrative position usually reserved for men who could prove descent from several generations of noblemen. Abbots, abbesses, and priors (those who administered monasteries and convents) were also subject to approval by the king. Again, these positions were usually held by noblemen, noblewomen, and other favorites of the king; and some offices were claimed by bishops who wanted extra income but who never lived in monasteries or performed any additional duties.

In short, the most lucrative positions in the French church were generally reserved for the younger sons of noblemen who, because of primogeniture, could not inherit their fathers' estate. As the historian John Lough observed in *An Introduction to Seventeenth Century France* (2nd ed., 1969),

> In a nobleman's family it was the recognized thing that the younger sons and daughters should be found a safe and comfortable existence in the Church. . . . The children of noblemen did not enter the Church because they felt it to be their true vocation. . . .

The result was that the highest posts in the Church were often filled by extraordinary misfits.

Clerics, like noblemen, were exempt from taxes (though the higher clergy would sometimes vote for voluntary contributions to the king), so taxes fell almost entirely on the working people. Those people, in addition to paying secular taxes (the most onerous direct tax was a land tax known as the *taille*), also paid a compulsory tithe to support the clergy—a tax that sometimes exceeded taxes paid to the state. John Lough said of the tithe,

> The method of collection was an additional source of grievance. As the tithe was a first charge on the crop, the collectors had to be informed in advance of the day when it was to be harvested. Meanwhile, until they arrived, the peasant was forbidden to remove his crop. When they came, they proceeded to take the pick of his produce and even carried off the straw, which the peasant could not well do without. To add to the peasant's resentment, tithes were often collected by a wealthy chapter or abbey, instead of going to maintain the poor *curé* and keep the parish church in a proper state of repair. Occasionally, indeed, the tithe . . . went to a layman.

With this cursory overview, we can better understand why Meslier condemned the French church as a branch of government that ruthlessly exploited the poor people of France. Meslier exempted some bishops and priests from his wrath, noting that they did their best to help the poor despite the thoroughly corrupt system in which they worked. But he also maintained that many members of the clergy were in it for the loot and pursued their own interests as much as any secular ruler or bureaucrat. Indeed, Meslier, speaking from his years of experience as a parish priest, recounted how many of his colleagues didn't believe what they preached any more than he did, and how they mocked their parishioners for their credulity:

> I was never able to take a liking to most of those good and hardy gentlemen who took such great pleasure in greedily receiving the fat payments for the vain functions of their ministry. I hated even more the mocking and clownish attitude of those other gentlemen who only think of having a good time with the large incomes of their good benefices and who among themselves cheerfully mock the mysteries, maxims, and the vain and deceitful ceremonies of their religion, and who even mock the simplicity of those who

believe and who in this belief supply them so piously and so lavishly to enjoy themselves and live so well at ease.

Since Meslier also believed that the "mysteries and mummeries" of the Christian religion are "things worthy of mockery and contempt," he did not fault others for agreeing with him on this point. What he had a problem with was the "burning, insatiable greed" found in fellow clerics who took advantage of "the public errors" to fatten their own purses, and who then mocked "the simplicity of those who are in ignorance and whom they themselves maintain in error." If clerics were able "to live so fatly and peacefully at the public expense," then the least they could do was to empathize with the dire circumstances of their parishioners and understand how uneducated peasants were especially liable to believe whatever they were told by religious authorities, however absurd those doctrines may have seemed to educated people. Clerics exhibit an "enormous ingratitude" and a "detestable treachery" when they "mock the simplicity" of the common people, "seeing that it is only from the work and sweat of the bodies of the poor that these men get all their livelihood and abundance."

That point brings us to an obvious problem, namely this: Given his long service as a parish priest, how did the atheist Meslier justify teaching doctrines that he personally regarded as false and even as absurd? I regard Meslier's thoughts on this topic, which appear in the second chapter of his *Testament*, as the most interesting part of the book. Although critics could easily charge Meslier with outright hypocrisy and dismiss his explanation as nothing more than a convenient rationalization, his account strikes me as a sincere effort to explain the situation in which he found himself. But however we may assess Meslier's explanation, it qualifies as a fascinating psychological document.

According to Meslier, "I was easily led in my youth to the ecclesiastical state to please my parents, who were pleased to see me there because it was a state of life softer, more peaceful and more honorable in the world than that of the common man." Was Meslier an atheist at that point? Unfortunately, he didn't say; but, at the very least, he apparently had strong doubts about the truth of Catholic doctrine: "I can truthfully say that the truth of any temporal advantage and the prospects of the fat payments of the ministry never brought me to love the duty of a profession so full of errors and impostures."

Meslier obviously felt guilty about teaching his parishioners doctrines that he himself regarded as ridiculous, so he offered a posthumous apology of sorts in his *Testament*:

> I declare to you that I was never without pain and extreme loathing for what I was doing. That is also why I totally hated all the vain functions of my ministry, and particularly all the idolatrous and superstitious celebrations of masses, and the vain and ridiculous administrations of sacraments that I had to do for you. I cursed them thousands of times to the core when I had to do them, and particularly when I had to do them with a little more attention and solemnity than normal when I saw you come to your churches with a little more devotion to attend some vain solemnities or to hear with a little more devotion what they make you believe to be the word of God, it seemed to me that I was abusing your good faith much more shamefully and that I was, consequently, much more worthy of reproach and condemnation, which increased my hatred of these kinds of ceremonies and pompous solemnities and vain functions of my ministry so much that I was hundreds and hundreds of times on the point of indiscreetly bursting

out with indignation, almost not able to hide my resentment any longer to keep to myself the indignation I felt. However, I did, in a way, keep it to myself, and I struggled to keep it to myself until the end of my days, not wanting to expose myself during my life to the indignation of the priests or to the cruelty of the tyrants who, it seemed to me, would not have found cruel enough tortures to punish me with for such so-called recklessness.

Meslier's fear of the legal consequences if he said what he truly believed or quit the priesthood was realistic. An apostate priest, especially an atheist, would have faced imprisonment at the very least, or he could have been sentenced to years as a galley slave or possibly executed. The prediction of many defenders of religious freedom, to the effect that the threat of persecution breeds hypocrisy among even good people who fear the legal consequences of intellectual candor, proved accurate in Meslier's case. He concealed his true beliefs and continued his career as a priest because he had no other option short of risking severe punishment. Meslier hoped his parishioners would sympathize with his plight, understand the dilemma in which he found himself, and appreciate how he attempted to make the best of a bad situation.

Meslier never solicited contributions from his flock; he never sought higher offices for financial gain or exploited the financial opportunities of his position; he never looked down on his parishioners or treated them with contempt; he helped them financially and in other ways whenever he could; he refrained from preaching the torments of hell and other especially absurd doctrines; and he used his pulpit to denounce the local lord for his cruelty. Meslier hoped his parishioners would remember these and other facts when they learned of his intellectual deceit.

> I am pleased, my dear friends, to die as peacefully as I lived. Moreover, having never given you any reason to want to harm me or to enjoy any harm that might come to me, I also do not believe that you would be happy to see me persecuted and tyrannized for this matter. That is why I resolved to keep silent until the end of my days.

Meslier left his *Testament* containing his real thoughts about religion because he had no fear of what might happen to him after his death. Heaven and hell were childish fictions. Death brings the total extinction of consciousness, so he could not be harmed or punished in any afterlife. Meslier therefore thumbed his nose at those who predicted that he would suffer in hell for his atheism:

> Let the priests, preachers, scholars, and all the instigators of such lies, errors, and impostures be scandalized as much as they want after my death; let them treat me, if they want, like an impious apostate, like a blasphemer and an atheist; let them insult me and curse me as they want. I do not really care since it will not bother me in the least.

Since Christian authorities sometimes exhumed and consigned to the flames the previously buried bodies of heretics, apostates, and disbelievers, Meslier sarcastically added that he couldn't care less what outraged authorities did with his body after his death:

> Likewise, let them do what they want with my body; let them tear it apart, cut it to pieces, roast it or fricassee it and then eat it, if they want, in whatever sauce they want, it will not trouble me at all. I will be entirely out of their reach; nothing will be able to frighten me.

These are remarkable statements, especially when we recall that Meslier was writing 300 years ago, in the early 18th century. He was clearly an extraordinary man.

20

Jean Meslier and Christian Ethics

In chapter 40 of his *Testament* ("Three Principal Errors of Christian Morality"), the atheist-priest Jean Meslier displayed a depth of criticism of Christianity that few free-thinkers have ever equaled, much less surpassed. This should come as no surprise to readers who make it to chapter 40, for in earlier chapters (especially chapter 33, "What Was His Preaching?"), Meslier accused Jesus of "malice and viciousness," even attributing to him "mental derangement."

> It is easy to see by all his speeches that Jesus Christ was really only a fool and a fanatic. And it is certain that if he came back again today among us, if it were

possible, and did and said the same things as before, we would certainly consider him nothing but a fool and fanatic.

This assessment runs contrary to the opinion of many early freethinkers, especially those English deists who expressed admiration for the moral teachings of Jesus and criticized later Christians for deviating from those teachings. But Meslier would have none of this, and his criticisms reflect a radical strain in French atheism that was largely (though not entirely) lacking in the English freethought tradition.

Meslier criticized the moral teachings of Christianity on three major points:

> The first is that it makes the perfection of virtue and the greatest good or advantage of man consist in the love and pursuit of pain and suffering according to the maxim of Christ, its chief, who said to his disciples that happy are the poor, happy are those who cry, who are hungry and thirsty, who suffer persecution for justice (Matt. 5:3–10). And according to other maxims of this Christ we have to carry our cross, renounce ourselves and all we possess, and if anyone wants to be perfect he has to sell everything he has and give it to the poor (Matt. 19:21; Luke 18:22).

Meslier, who lived with the poor during his decades as a parish priest, saw nothing virtuous or admirable in poverty, especially when that poverty resulted from exploitation by the powerful. It is "clearly an error and madness to say that the greatest good and happiness of man consists in weeping and groaning, in being poor and unhappy, hungry and thirsty, etc." Of course, Meslier understood that Christians did not preach poverty and suffering for their own sakes; rather, they claimed that the poor and suffering will be rewarded in an afterlife. But this teaching was "absolutely false," according to Meslier. This life is all there is; the "so-called kingdom of heaven, which our superstitious god-cultists seem to make such a big deal about, is only an imaginary kingdom." The desire for pleasure and a good life is part of human nature, so it is an abuse to teach the ignorant to "love and pursue real pain and suffering on the pretext of acquiring lovely rewards that are only imaginary." The teachings that pain and suffering will be rewarded in an afterlife, and that we should renounce everything we possess, "is based only on the word of a miserable fanatic," Jesus; and it is "an error and madness in men to want to follow or put any faith in such a maxim that is so contrary to the good of Nature and good judgment."

Meslier's comments on this matter were closely related to his belief that governments and churches teach the virtues of poverty and suffering as a means to keep the poor in their place, while expropriating from the poor the fruits of their labor. The doctrine of an afterlife served as an ideological smokescreen for political control and exploitation.

Meslier's second criticism focused on what he viewed as the Christian bias against innocent sexuality, and especially the condemnation not only of overt deeds but of sexual thoughts and feelings as well, if those thoughts and feelings occur outside the context of marriage. Nothing is more natural to man than sexuality, and to condemn this natural impulse as sinful and worthy of hellfire is to condemn an essential aspect of human nature, one rooted in "the most intimate depths" of our being. Would an infinitely good God really want "to make young people burn eternally in the dreadful flames of hell only for having had a few moments of pleasure together? . . . Or even only for having consented and indulged in thoughts, desires, or carnal motions that God himself had formed and aroused in them?" To attribute such intentions to a perfect and infinitely good God is "entirely ridiculous and absurd and . . . disgraceful. . . . The thought alone of such cruelty is monstrous."

Before we accuse Meslier of favoring unbridled libertinism—an accusation commonly hurled against early atheists and other freethinkers—we need to keep in mind that he disapproved of "the debauchery of men or women who would indiscreetly or excessively abandon themselves to this animal inclination." Meslier condemned "this excess and disorder as well as all other kinds of excess and disorder." People should conform to the "laws, customs, and practices" of the countries in which they live. Meslier simply wished to protest the Christian doctrine that sexual "actions, desires, or thoughts and indulgences are crimes worthy of eternal punishments and torments." Sexual excesses are ultimately slight and trivial human failings; to teach that a wise and benevolent deity would punish people severely for such actions is at once absurd and disgraceful.

Meslier's third objection to Christian ethics (as taught by Jesus) is in some ways the most interesting of the lot:

> Here again is another error of this Christian moral-
> ity: it teaches that we must love our enemies, not take
> revenge for injuries and not even resist vicious men,
> but, on the contrary, that we must bless those who
> curse us, do good to those who do us harm, let them
> rob us when they want to take what we have, and
> always quietly suffer the injuries and mistreatments
> that they do, etc.

These teachings, according to Meslier, are contrary to "natural right and reason."

> It is obviously a natural right, natural reason, natural equality and justice to preserve our life and goods against those who want to take them from us unjustly. And as it is natural to hate evil, it is also natural to hate those who unjustly do evil. Now, the aforementioned maxims of Christian morality go directly against all these natural rights and, consequently, are false. And it is an error to want to teach them and make people practice them, seeing that they are contrary to all natural rights and that they clearly tend to the reversal of justice, to the oppression of the poor and weak, and they are contrary to the good government of men.

Here again Meslier criticized "maxims of the Christian religion" because they "clearly tend to favor the vicious and their oppression of the good and the weak." The doctrine that we should love our enemies and not resist or seek revenge against those who harm us has benefited rulers who "boldly attack the good and do whatever they want without punishment and without fear." Meslier repudiated the doctrine of passive obedience unequivocally. Throughout the *Testament*, he endorsed violent resistance against tyrannical rulers and their unjust actions. Indeed, in chapter 2, we find the first formulation of a saying that has commonly been attributed to the French atheist Denis Diderot (1713–1784): "Men will never be free until the last king is strangled with the entrails of the last priest." Meslier shared the sentiment but did not take credit for the idea. He referred, instead, to a common Frenchman "who had no culture or education" but who had the sound judgment to understand the evils inflicted on him and other poor people by the French government and Gallican Church:

> In his wish and in his way of expressing his thought it seemed that he saw rather far and penetrated rather deeply into the detestable mystery of iniquity of which I just spoke, and recognized very well the perpetrators and instigators. His wish was that all the rulers of the earth and all the nobles be hanged and strangled with the guts of priests.

This expression, Meslier remarked, "may seem hard, rude, and shocking, but you must admit that it is candid and simple." It also expresses, if crudely, what rulers deserve for their merciless exploitation of the ruled. If Meslier could have been granted a single wish, he would have wished for the strength, courage, and resolve of Hercules so that he could "have the pleasure of bludgeoning all the monster tyrants with their crowned heads and all the other monsters and ministers of errors and iniquity who make all the people of the earth groan so piteously." Since Meslier did not believe in hell, he did not agree with those Christians who believed that tyrants will suffer eternal torment for their crimes, however comfortable their life on earth may be. He preferred to see rulers punished in this life at the hands of their victims. Meslier did not reserve justice and revenge for a god in whom he did not believe.

21

The Political Theory of Jean Meslier

In his lengthy article "Jean Meslier and the 'Gentle Inclination of Nature'," the French philosopher Michel Onfray
characterized Meslier as "Atheist, deChristianizer, anarchist,
communist, materialist, internationalist, revolutionary, [and]
leftist." That is quite a bundle of labels; and given Onfray's
widely acknowledged expertise on Meslier, it is risky to challenge his judgments about the atheist-priest. But Onfray is
himself a left-anarchist; and, in my judgment, he occasionally
succumbs to the natural tendency to find heroic precursors to
his own views, even when that involves reading more into a
text than is actually there. Onfray is aware of this tendency—
as is evident from his observation: "In 1919 the Bolsheviks

engrave his name on an obelisk in Moscow. Meslier becomes a precursor enrolled in the Soviet adventure!"[26]

In his classic study, *The Great Anarchists: Ideas and Teachings of Seven Major Thinkers*, Paul Eltzbacher divided anarchism into two basic types: *communist* and *individualist* anarchism. As Eltzbacher—an individualist anarchist in the school of Benjamin Tucker—noted, "Anarchistic teachings have in common only this, that they negate the State for our future."[27] Now, since Michel Onfray dubbed Meslier a communist *and* an anarchist, we should begin with the question of whether Meslier was an anarchist at all. Although Meslier vehemently criticized the French monarchy and other governments of his day, condemning them as engines of despotism and ruthless exploiters of the poor, it does not follow that he endorsed the anarchist teaching that *all* governments are necessarily unjust and should be abolished. (Of course, our opinion about this issue will depend on how we define "government" and "state.")

So, was Meslier an anarchist? I find nothing in his *Testament* to support the claim that he was. On the contrary, Meslier repeatedly affirmed the need for just governments that pursue the common good rather than the private good of privileged groups. He believed, for example, that "all well-ruled republics need experts to teach virtue and to instruct men in good manners as well as the arts and sciences." If anything, this and similar remarks indicate that Meslier wished to assign to his ideal government powers that modern libertarians would reject, especially in the field of education. Children should "all be raised, nourished, and supported in common with public and common goods." Similarly, they should "be equally well educated in good manners and honesty, as well as in the arts and sciences, as much as necessary and suitable for each with respect to usefulness for the public and the need that it could have of their service." By educating all children "in the same principles of morality and rules of propriety and honesty, it would be easy to make them all wise and honest, to make them all work together and tend to the same good and make them all capable of usefully serving their country. This would certainly be advantageous for the public good and human society." In contrast, educational diversity "inspires in men only opposition and different temperaments, opinions, and sentiments, which makes them unable to tolerate one another peaceably and, consequently, to agree with others unanimously about the same good, which is a cause of continual troubles and divisions among them."

Although these passages do not explicitly call for the *state* to provide an education that is at once universal and uniform, a secular state system is almost certainly what Meslier had in mind. The same proposal would later become standard fare among French *philosophes* and freethinkers, and this widespread call for state education was one of the most anti-libertarian aspects of Enlightenment thought. No self-respecting anarchist would agree with the proposal to place education in the hands of the state, nor would most anarchists agree with Meslier that education should be the same for all children. In the view of William Godwin, Benjamin Tucker, and other prominent anarchists, entrusting the state with the job of teaching values to children is like entrusting the fox to guard the henhouse. As Godwin put it in *Enquiry Concerning Political Justice* (3rd ed., 1797), "Government will not fail to employ [education] to strengthen its hands, and perpetuate its institutions."

Elsewhere in the *Testament*, Meslier clearly expressed his belief that an orderly society requires some measure of political authority:

> All men are equal by nature; they all hold equally the right to live and to walk upon the earth, the right to enjoy their natural liberty and to share in the goods of the land, with everyone working usefully to have the things that are necessary and useful in life. But, since they live in society and since a society or community of men cannot be ruled well or sustained in good

order without some kind of dependence and subordination between them, it is absolutely for the good of
human society that there be some kind of dependence
and subordination among them.

That is the language of a defender of government, not the
language of an anarchist. Meslier demanded only that a government "be just and well proportioned, i.e., that it should
not exalt some and debase others, flatter some and trample
others, give to some and leave nothing for others. . . ." Similar
statements recur throughout the *Testament*, so how Michel
Onfray reached the conclusion that Meslier was an anarchist
remains a puzzle to me.

Let us now turn to the question of whether Meslier, if not
an anarchist, was a communist of some kind. Before proceeding, however, I should point out that the *Testament*, written over a period of 10 years while Meslier was in his 50s,
is disorganized and repetitive, and it sometimes substitutes
over-the-top polemicism for reasoned arguments. Meslier
apologized for some of these flaws, explaining that he wrote
the *Testament* in bits and pieces, when he could find free
time from his priestly duties. In some respects, therefore, the
Testament resembles an intellectual journal more than a pol-
ished manuscript. As a result, even careful readers are bound

to feel frustrated when attempting to understand Meslier's position on some important controversies. We should keep this difficulty in mind while exploring the issue of whether "communism" is an appropriate label for Meslier's ideas about property.

"Communism" is a highly charged label, one brimming with negative connotations. But if we strip the term down to bare essentials and use it to signify *only* the doctrine that all or most goods should be the common property of society rather than individually owned, then there may be some justification in dubbing Meslier a communist. I say there *may* be some justification because Meslier was unclear about some key features of his political philosophy. In the final analysis, I think it would be incorrect to identify Meslier's ideas about property as communistic.

Consider Meslier's comments about the French nobility, in chapter 43 of the *Testament*. Meslier asserted that the first nobles were "bloody and cruel people, thieves and parricides" who acquired and sustained their privileged status by brute force. Thus, instead of glorifying the nobility, the French people "should rather be ashamed of such a criminal and hateful birth and source, and the people should only have hatred and aversion for them." The class system in France "clearly puts all the authority, all the goods, pleasures, satisfactions, wealth, and even the idleness on the side of the rulers, the rich, and the nobles, and puts on the side of the poor everything that is painful and distressing." Note that Meslier condemns "the rich," along with rulers and nobles, as exploiters of the poor. How should this inclusion be understood? Should we interpret Meslier to mean that wealth, per se, can only be acquired at the expense of the poor? Modern socialists and communists would probably favor that *economic* interpretation, since it would corroborate their own belief in economic exploitation and class struggle. More plausible, in my judgment, would be to understand Meslier as condemning *only* those people who acquired their wealth by the *political* means of state coercion.

My interpretation, if correct, would mean that Meslier did not object to wealth earned through voluntary market transactions; rather, his targets were those state functionaries who became rich by plundering the public via taxes and tithes, along with those merchants and manufacturers who benefited from state-granted monopolies and other privileges. The "rich" are mentioned again in this passage from the same paragraph:

> The disproportion is all the more unjust and detestable for the people since it makes them entirely dependent on the nobles and the rich, and it makes them,

so to speak, their slaves, to the point of making them suffer not only their put-downs, scorn, and abuse, but also their persecution, injustice, and mistreatment.

Again, we must ask, What did Meslier mean by "the rich"? In the course of explaining his position, Meslier quoted the following passage from another writer—the anonymous author of a book titled *Letters Writ by a Turkish Spy.*

There is nothing so vile and so abject, nothing so poor and despicable as the peasantry of France. Moreover, they work only for the rulers and the nobles, and with all their work they still have great trouble to earn enough bread for themselves. In a word, the peasants are absolutely the slaves of the rulers and nobles, whose lands they give value to and from whom they rent their farms. They are no less oppressed by the public taxes and the salt taxes than by the individual burdens that their masters impose on them, without even considering what the clergy unjustly demand of these poor unfortunates.

Here the exploiting class is expressly identified as those who make money through the coercive mechanism of government. Thus, given Meslier's scathing denunciations of taxes, it is reasonable to conclude that his condemnation of the "rich" pertained specifically to those members of the ruling class who acquired their wealth through taxes, tithes, and other governmental revenues coercively extracted from the ruled. But Meslier never explicitly distinguished between the economic and political means of acquiring wealth, so a certain amount of guesswork is required to reach this conclusion.

On the other side of the ledger, we have Meslier's criticisms of private property. For example, we see his approval of Blaise Pascal's contention that "the usurpation of all lands and the evils that ensued came only from the fact that each individual wanted to appropriate for himself the things that should have been left in common." Likewise, the "divine Plato" banished from his utopia the words "mine" and "thine"—"judging rightly that so long as there was something to divvy up, there would always be dissatisfaction, which breeds troubles, divisions, wars, and lawsuits."

Elsewhere in the *Testament*, Meslier wrote,

> In brief, if all the goods . . . were wisely governed and dispensed, no one would have to fear drought or poverty for themselves or their families, since all the goods and riches would exist equally for everyone, which would certainly be the greatest good and happiness that could happen to men.

The key question about such passages, which recur at various places in the *Testament*, is whether Meslier thought that the economic equality he desired should be brought about by voluntary means, or whether such equality should be coercively imposed by government. I take up this problem, which is essential to determining whether or not Meslier qualified as a "communist" in any significant sense of the word, in the next chapter.

22

Jean Meslier on Property

In the penultimate chapter of his *Testament*, the atheist-priest Jean Meslier wrote this:

> You and your descendants will always be miserable and unhappy . . . as long as there is such a great and enormous disproportion of states and conditions; as long as you do not possess and enjoy in common the goods of the earth; as long as the good and bad and the pains of life are so badly shared among you, since it is not at all just that some bear all the pains of labor and all the discomforts of life while others enjoy alone without pain or labor all the goods and comforts of life.

Meslier's belief that people should "possess and enjoy in common the goods of the earth" raises the question of whether he advocated a type of communism, as Michel Onfray and other interpreters have maintained. When I wrote the previous chapter, I believed that although there may be "some justification" for ascribing communistic ideas to Meslier, "I think it would be incorrect to identify Meslier's ideas about property as communistic." Now, having reread Meslier's remarks about property—this time with more care—I feel I must revise that conclusion. Meslier's ideas may indeed be described as communistic, but only in the older meaning of the term.

That revision raises two issues. First, Meslier's comments about property are fragmentary and, at times, inconsistent; they certainly don't qualify as a *theory* of property, so it is difficult to reach a definitive conclusion. Second, labeling his comments about property "communistic" will almost certainly mislead those readers who associate communism with a strong, authoritarian state. Although, as I explained previously, Meslier was no anarchist, neither was he a cheerleader for strong, expansive central government. His criticisms of taxes and tax collectors were unrelenting, as were his assaults on the French bureaucracy and other state functionaries who enforced the will of the sovereign. Again and again, Meslier attacked the predatory class of French officials (including the clergy) who lived off the labor of the working class while producing nothing themselves.

Nevertheless, Meslier's position on property may be described as communistic in the same way that this label has been applied to early Christian communities in the Roman Empire. The *ideal* of common property, in contrast to private property, was advocated for many centuries by leading Catholic theologians. The eminent historian Ernest Barker wrote the following in his introduction to *The Social and Political Ideas of Some Great Medieval Thinkers* (ed. Hearnshaw, 1923):

> It had been a general doctrine in the Church since the days of St. Augustine that communism was the ideal condition of society; and the great canonist Gratian is following tradition when he writes "by the law of nature all things are the common property of all men"—a principle followed by the primitive Church in Jerusalem, and taught by Plato.

According to Meslier, "In all appearances the Christian religion in the beginning wanted its followers to restore this way of living in common, as if it were the best and most suitable for men." Meslier then quoted one of two passages in the Acts of the Apostles (2:44-45, RSV) that were frequently cited by advocates of Christian communism. After the apostle Peter had baptized around 3,000 people and formed the first Christian community in Jerusalem, "all who believed were together and had all things in common; and they sold their possessions and goods and distributed them to all, as any had need." A similar passage occurs a little later, in Acts 4:32, 34–37:

> Now the company of those who believed were of one heart and soul, and no one said that any of the things which he possessed was his own, but they had everything in common. . . . There was not a needy person among them, for as many as were possessors of lands or houses sold them, and brought the proceeds of what was sold, and laid it at the apostles' feet; and distribution was made to each as any had need. Thus Joseph, who was surnamed by the apostles Barnabas . . . sold a field which belonged to him, and brought the money and laid it at the apostles' feet.

Meslier believed that this arrangement "did not last so long among [Christians] because greed slipped into their hearts and soon broke up this common union of goods and set division among them as it was before." Nevertheless, the ideal of common property survived in monasteries, and this is why monks "are always kept in such a thriving condition that they lack nothing and never feel the miseries or discomforts of poverty, which makes most men so unhappy in life." Indeed, if monks ever "stopped possessing their goods in common and began sharing them so that each one of them enjoyed their share separately as seemed good to them, they would soon be like the others exposed and reduced to all the miseries and discomforts of life." The monastic practice of holding all goods in common should serve as a model for French society in general:

It would certainly be the same with all the parishes if the people there wanted to agree to live peaceably together in common, to all work usefully in common and to enjoy equally in common each in their district, the goods of the land and the fruits of their labor. . . . They could, if they wanted, in this way of living in common, obtain everywhere an abundance of all goods and thus protect themselves from all the miseries and discomforts of poverty, which would empower them all to live happily and contently instead of enjoying separately, as they do, all the goods of the land and commodities of life and being exposed to and dragged into all kinds of evils and miseries. . . . So, it is clearly an abuse, and a very great abuse in them to possess separately, as they each do, the goods and commodities of life and to enjoy them separately, since they are deprived of so many great benefits and are exposed to and dragged into so many great evils and miseries.

Although the passages from Acts (quoted above) were frequently cited by later proponents of Christian communism and socialism, it is important to note that they describe a *voluntary* pooling of resources among the members of a relatively small community. No coercion, and certainly no coercion by a government, was recommended or sanctioned. Nor is private property, per se, attacked in those passages; on the contrary, the reference to Joseph Barnabas says that he "sold a field which belonged to him," suggesting that he had legitimate title to that land.

A number of church fathers noted the voluntary activities of early Christian communities. For example, Tertullian (c. 155–240) observed that all institutions of the Roman government, even its charities, were based on coercion. Among Christians, in contrast, "everything is voluntary." The church did not rely on coercive taxation; Christians contributed voluntarily "to support the destitute, and to pay for their burial expenses; to supply the needs of boys and girls lacking money and power, and of old people confined to the home." Christians "do not hesitate to share our earthly goods with one another." Early Christians with wealth often sold their personal property and donated the proceeds to a common fund that was distributed to other Christians, according to need. There was no suggestion that such donors did not justly own the property they decided to sell, or that private property itself is the product of exploitation.

Did Meslier's ideal society, like that of the early Christians, involve a *voluntary* system of communal property? It is difficult to answer that question with certainty. Throughout the *Testament*, Meslier insisted that the worker who produces a good should have the right to dispose of that good for his own benefit and decried the grave injustice of expropriating the fruits of his labor. In that context, Meslier appeared to advocate a purely voluntary system of communal property—a system in which private goods are voluntarily converted into common goods because of the (supposed) economic advantages of the latter system, as when a destitute person may draw from a common stock of resources rather than starve.

But matters become considerably more cloudy when we learn the details of Meslier's ideal society. In chapter 48 of the *Testament*, Meslier expressly condemned the "individual appropriation" of property—a position that is difficult to reconcile with other statements in his book. Instead of individual appropriation, people should possess property in common and enjoy that property in common. Meslier proposed a decentralized system of common ownership, one centered in local communities—"the same city, town, village, or parish." The inhabitants of these communities may be regarded as members of the same family, as brothers and sisters who have "the same or similar food and being all equally well clothed, well housed, well bedded, and well heated, and applying themselves also equally to the labor, i.e., to the work or to some honest and useful job, everyone pursuing his profession or what would be most necessary or most appropriate according to the time and season and the possible need for certain things." These communities would not be under the "leadership of those who may want to dominate haughtily and tyrannically over the others, but under the leadership and direction of those who are the wisest and have the best intentions for the advancement and maintenance of the public good." These communities would form alliances with other communities for the sake of peace and to provide mutual aid in time of need.

As we dig deeper into Meslier's scheme for an ideal society, it becomes evident that coercion would be necessary to implement his utopia. And it is perfectly correct to describe Meslier's social plan as utopian, especially given his repeated assertions that all misery, want, and exploitation would disappear if only people, suitably educated, would adopt reason as their guide instead of succumbing to the false and absurd claims of religion. (I daresay that Meslier could have learned some important things about human nature and avoided making some boneheaded claims if he had taken more seriously the insights of the better Christian philosophers and theologians.) Meslier's call for a communistic utopia was nothing new; similar ideas are found in the writings of Plato, Thomas More, and others. The main difference between Meslier's utopia and those proposed by earlier writers lies in Meslier's rejection of a centralized authority that plans and directs the activities and institutions of an entire society. Meslier proposed instead a federation of smaller communities, but this was a distinction without a difference so far as the need to coerce unwilling participants is concerned.

Consider one of the more disturbing passages in the *Testament.* Despite his praise of the common property found in monasteries, Meslier detested monks, especially those mendicants who begged for their food and other necessities. Now, we might think that soliciting voluntary contributions would, in principle, be unobjectionable for a philosopher with libertarian proclivities. But monks, according to Meslier, produced nothing of social value, so he would have forbidden this practice and *forced* monks to do what he deemed honest labor:

> The profession of priests, and particularly of monks,
> is nothing but a profession of errors, superstitions,
> and impostures and, consequently, far from being

a profession considered useful and necessary in a good and wise republic, it should, on the contrary be regarded as harmful and pernicious. And so, instead of rewarding the people of such a profession, we should rather absolutely forbid all the superstitious and abusive functions of their ministry and absolutely force them to do some honest and useful work like others.

Something is clearly out of whack in Meslier's version of a free and enlightened society.

The Christian Theory
of Property

In the previous chapter, I discussed Jean Meslier's defense of common property over private property. Although Meslier was an atheist who repudiated many of Christianity's metaphysical and ethical teachings, his position on property was in some respects curiously similar to that of traditional Christianity, especially as found in the writings of the church fathers, such as Ambrose (340–397) and Augustine (354–430). The theory of private property found in most classical liberal texts—such as John Locke's claim that we originally acquire ownership of a natural resource by "mixing" our labor with it—was not accepted by leading Christian theologians for many centuries. Contrary to Locke, according to whom private property is a natural right, Augustine and other Christians typically argued that private property is not sanctioned by the original natural law; rather, it is a creation of government. Thus, in the early fifth century, when the Christian schismatics known as Donatists complained that the orthodox Christian government of Imperial Rome had confiscated their property without just cause—property that they had earned by their labor—Augustine replied that Romans enjoyed their property solely on the sufferance of the Roman government, who could confiscate that property at its own discretion. Romans had rights in private property only because the government permitted it, so when it rescinded those rights the victims had no legitimate complaint. According to Augustine, there is no such thing as a natural right to private property that a government has a duty to respect.

To understand Augustine's position we need to appreciate the standard Christian doctrine of original sin. Human nature before Adam's fall into sin—known as *prelapsarian* man—was perfect, having been created in God's image. It was only *after* Adam's fall into sin that human nature became vitiated with the evil and destructive tendencies, such as avarice, selfishness, and violence, that we know today. Thus, if the fall had never occurred, three institutions would have been unnecessary and would never have arisen: private property, government, and slavery. These institutions were instituted and sanctioned by God solely because of original sin; they were intended, as Augustine put it, as a *punishment* and *remedy* for sin. Every church father who wrote about property agreed with this position. Common property, not private property, would have been the rule in the idyllic Garden of Eden if Adam had never sinned and if humans had remained in their pure, prelapsarian condition. Prelapsarian man would not have been tainted with the acquisitive and violent tendencies of postlapsarian man, so the coercive institutions of private property, government, and slavery would have been unknown.

According to Alexander J. Carlyle, a distinguished historian of medieval political thought, the Christian theory of property "is the opposite of that of Locke, that private property is an institution of natural law, and arises out of labour."

To the Fathers the only natural condition is that of common ownership and individual use. The world was made for the common benefit of mankind, that all should receive from it what they require. They admit, however, that human nature being what it is, greedy, avaricious, and vicious, it is impossible for men to live normally under the condition of common ownership. This represents the more perfect way of life, and this principle was represented in the organization of the monastic life, as it generally took shape. For mankind in general, some organization of ownership became necessary, and this was provided by the State and its laws, which have decided the conditions and limitations of ownership. Private property is therefore practically the creation of the State, and is defined, limited, and changed by the State.[28]

Christian theologians did not oppose private property, government, or slavery. On the contrary, these institutions were specifically mandated and authorized by God for corrupt human beings, even though they were not part of the original, or primitive, natural law. Charles H. McIlwain explained this point in his classic work, *The Growth of Political Thought in the West*:

The corruption of man began with the fall, and that corruption, the inheritance of all the children of Adam, created for the human race the necessity for coercive law and other like institutions. To supply the need God gave man the Mosaic law, and sanctioned human laws and institutions necessary to curb the evils arising from avarice, violence, and other forms of vice. Coercive law . . . is no part of man's original nature; it came as a corrective of conditions arising from man's fall from innocence. It is no branch of the law of nature . . . but it is none the less provided by the ordinance or sanction of God as a partial remedy for the consequences of that sin, and to this extent has a divine origin and a divine character. Its precepts must therefore be obeyed as a religious obligation. "Wherefore ye must needs be in subjection, not only because of the wrath, but also for conscience' sake. (Romans xiii.)"[29]

Jean Meslier, in effect, accepted the Christian teaching about the existence of common property in a prelapsarian society; but, having rejected the doctrine of original sin, he did not accept the Christian argument that private property was needed because of a corrupted human nature generated by Adam's fall. His stance resembles the position adopted by some radical Protestant sects during the 17th century, such as the Family of Love and the Grindletonians, "who taught that prelapsarian perfection could be attained in this life."[30] Without sin, private property would be unnecessary and undesirable, so such groups typically advocated a return to the primitive communism of prelapsarian man. Private property would be inappropriate in a community of saints; common property was the ideal.

As Ludwig von Mises noted in *Socialism: An Economic and Sociological Analysis*, many ancient civilizations believed in the "romantic Utopia of common ownership."

> In ancient Rome it was the legend of the Golden Age of Saturn, described in glowing terms by Virgil, Tibullus, and Ovid, and praised by Seneca. Those were the carefree, happy days when none had private property and all prospered in the bounty of a generous Nature. Modern Socialism, of course, imagines itself beyond such simplicity and childishness, but its dreams differ little from those of the Imperial Romans.[31]

The early Christian conception of a Golden Age was profoundly influenced by the writings of the Roman philosopher Seneca, a leading Stoic. Christians took the sketchy account of the Garden of Eden in Genesis and fleshed it out with the more elaborate description of the Golden Age found in the Letters of Seneca. Seneca, referring to men in the primitive Golden Age, wrote this:

> What race of men could be luckier? Share and share alike they enjoyed nature. She saw to each and every

man's requirements for survival like a parent. What it all amounted to was undisturbed possession of resources owned by the community. I can surely call that race of men one of the unparalleled riches, it being impossible to find a single pauper.[32]

Before avarice burst on the scene—which caused people to claim exclusive property in land and other goods, and to covet luxury items that were unnecessary to fulfill their real needs—scarcity, competition for resources, and violent conflicts were nonexistent.

The earth herself, untilled, was more productive, her yields being more than ample for the needs of peoples who did not raid each other. . . . All was equally divided among people, living in complete harmony. The stronger had not yet started laying hands on the weaker; the avaricious person had not yet started hiding things away, to be hoarded for his own use, so shutting the next man off from actual necessities of life; each cared as much about the other as about himself. Weapons were unused; hands still unstained with human blood had directed their hostility exclusively against wild beasts.[33]

The early Christian view of property held sway for many centuries, though it was modified somewhat after the writings of Aristotle were rediscovered in the 12th century. When Thomas Aquinas (1225–1274), having integrated many of Aristotle's ideas into his writings, discussed property, he treated it as more of a natural institution than had many previous theologians. Nevertheless, Aquinas agreed that common ownership was the original condition of humankind, and this led him to argue that though the acquisition of property fulfills a natural need, such property (beyond what is needed for one's personal use) is legitimate only when devoted to the common good.

Thus, we see how the prelapsarian notion of common property influenced Christian thinking about the proper uses of private property. Common property, though a thing of the past, remained an ideal in the Christian theory of private property; it served as a beacon indicating the proper use of privately owned wealth. Beyond what was needed to satisfy the legitimate needs of the owner, private property could be justified only if the owner devoted it, not to his own selfish benefit and pleasure, but to furthering the common good. This was the original purpose of common property in prelapsarian society, after all, so the system of private property should emulate that function as much as possible.

The traditional Christian theory of private property differed substantially from the theory embraced by most classical liberals and libertarians, whose approach may broadly be described as secular. The nature of those differences is the topic of the next chapter.

Early Christianity and the Modern Libertarian Movement

In the previous chapter, I explained the traditional Christian theory of private property. According to every church father and most Christian theologians during the Middle Ages, common property was the original social condition of humankind before Adam's fall into sin. Prelapsarian man was not corrupted by the evil tendencies of avarice, violence, and the lust for power and domination over others. Only when those impulses, which resulted from original sin, became interwoven into the nature of postlapsarian man did the institutions of private property, government, and slavery become necessary as a punishment and remedy for sin. These institutions were specifically mandated by God to hold the evil tendencies of a degenerate human nature in check; they were necessary preconditions of social order.

As I have repeatedly noted, private property was not the only institution that resulted from original sin. Government and slavery were also included in the standard account. It is fairly easy to understand how government fits into the abstract scheme of prelapsarian versus postlapsarian man. More difficult to understand is how slavery was justified as part of the theory of original sin. This topic requires more space and attention to details than I can give it here, so I will dance around the topic in an effort to make a more general point, without addressing the problem of slavery directly.

The Christian defense of slavery and other atrocities is a controversial topic, one that may offend the sensibilities of those conservatives who insist that America's freedom was founded on "Judeo-Christian values." In response, freethinkers have pointed out that for many centuries, leading Christian thinkers defended slavery, religious persecution, and sundry other evils. Responding to that point, Christians have distinguished between the repulsive ideas endorsed by some individual Christians throughout history and the authentic Christian ideas authorized by the Bible—the revealed Word of God.

Although this explanation leaves many questions unanswered, it should be accepted, in general terms, with grace by atheists, for atheists have been victims of the selfsame abuse at the hands of their Christian critics. I cannot count the number of times I have encountered the argument that atheistic values must favor communism over freedom: was not atheism the official position of the Soviet Union? The absurdity of this style of argument, whether directed against Christians or atheists, is obvious when represented without frills; but the same style of argument, when dressed to the nines, will often pass without notice. One need only watch some panel discussions on Fox News, or some interviews and speeches with Republican presidential candidates, to find examples.

The basic point I wish to make here has to do with the strenuous efforts made by theologians over many centuries to render Christianity an *internally consistent system of thought*, or worldview. However irrational Christian ideology may appear to freethinkers and other outsiders, to insiders it appears in a more favorable light. To one who accepts the elementary tenets of Christianity, the various fine points of theology—especially as developed by Thomism (the ideas of Thomas Aquinas) and Scholasticism generally—appear as finely honed links that connect different ideas together to form a tightly integrated system of thought. This has always been the main appeal of philosophical *systems*, whether religious *or* secular. When Enlightenment philosophers expressly repudiated philosophical system-building, insisting instead that philosophy should be done piecemeal, they put themselves at a serious disadvantage relative to religious systems of thought. When you adhere to an *internally coherent system of thought*—whether religious or secular—the world will make much more sense to you, even if the component parts, when considered separately, make little sense at all.

Religious systems of thought have their own disadvantages, however, especially when a given system is based on the Bible or on some other source of special revelation. A foundation that lays claim to divine inspiration remains fixed, and this feature makes it highly vulnerable to external attacks. If one brick is removed from a static and unalterable system of thought, the entire structure, unable to adjust to the external threat, may collapse. This problem has arisen many times when freethinkers have criticized Christianity.

Consider the popular claim that Christianity is morally superior to other philosophies. An obvious problem arises when this claim is joined to a serious commitment to the Bible as divinely inspired, because few if any self-identified Christians endorse everything taught and justified in the Bible. Notable exceptions are abundant in the Old Testament, such as the authorization of human sacrifices (Lev. 27:28–29; Judg. 11:29–40; 2 Sam. 21:1–9). Yahweh—the national god of Israel and Judah—is reported to have killed the first-born of every Egyptian family (Exod. 12:29). In addition, he sanctioned slavery (Exod. 21:2–6; Lev. 25:44–46) and the selling of one's daughter (Exod. 21:7). Yahweh commanded the killing of witches (Exod. 22:18), death for heresy (Exod. 22:20), death for violating the Sabbath (Exod. 31:14–15), death for cursing one's parents (Lev. 20:9), death for adultery (Lev. 20:10), death for blasphemy (Lev. 24:16), and death by stoning for unchastity at the time of marriage—a penalty imposed only on women (Deut. 22:20–21).

Yahweh sometimes exterminated large numbers of people, usually through pestilence or famine, and often for rather unusual offenses. In one strange case, he is reported to have killed 70,000 men because David took a census of Israel (2 Sam. 24); and according to another story, Yahweh sent two bears to rip apart 42 children who mocked the prophet Elisha (2 Kings 2:23–24).

These and similar passages, mainly from the Old Testament, provided deists and other freethinkers with an abundance of ammunition in their crusade against Christianity. That ammunition proved especially useful when responding to the common argument that Judeo-Christian values are essential to social order and the cultivation of moral virtue—an argument that, in turn, was used to justify the persecution of atheists, who supposedly posed a serious threat to the moral foundations of civilization.

The aforementioned biblical passages I cited were what Thomas Jefferson had in mind when he called the god of the Old Testament "a being of terrific character—cruel, vindictive, capricious, and unjust." They also inspired Thomas Paine to write polemical denunciations of the Bible. Here is a typical passage from Paine's notorious attack on Christianity, *The Age of Reason*, a classic of freethought literature that has probably been read by more people than any other book of its type:

> Whenever we read the obscene stories, the voluptuous debaucheries, the cruel and torturous executions, the unrelenting vindictiveness, with which more than half the Bible is filled, it would be more consistent that we called it the word of a demon, than the word of God. It is a history of wickedness, that has served to corrupt and brutalize mankind; and, for my part, I sincerely detest it, as I detest everything that is cruel.

Over the centuries, Christians found ways to deal with the problem of unsavory Old Testament passages. A common and reasonable explanation (from a theological perspective) is that most of the Old Testament precepts and commands, a significant portion of which are clustered in Leviticus, were limited, context-bound prescriptions and proscriptions that God intended solely for the ancient Jews. With the obvious exception of the Decalogue (the Ten Commandments), those ceremonial rules and tribal laws are not part of the natural law; they are not part of the system of moral precepts, knowable to reason, that apply universally to every human being. Indeed, in the New Testament both Jesus and Paul declared that the Old Law is no longer applicable, that it has been superseded or fulfilled by the New Law of Christ, as we find in John 13:34–33. Jesus says,

> A new commandment I give to you, that you love one another, as I have loved you, that you will also love one another. By this all will know that you are My disciples, if you have love for one another.

This and similar passages were frequently invoked by Christian defenders of religious freedom who were astonished by the standard Christian arguments in favor of persecution. How was it possible, these pro-freedom Christians asked, to justify persecution in the name of Christ, or to demand conformity in some fine points of theology, such as the Trinity, that were never mentioned by Jesus or, for that matter, anywhere in the New Testament?

Deists had a point when they argued that the persecuting spirit of Christianity was the consequence of needless theological blunders, and that religious conformity, coercively imposed, could not be justified by the moral teachings of Jesus. Nevertheless, as Christianity grew in numbers and influence and had to compete with other religious groups, a technical theology (which is essentially philosophy applied to divine matters) was bound to develop; and with it came the inevitable disagreements among Christians themselves.

A parallel may be drawn here with modern libertarianism, which, like early Christianity, is heavily infused with ideology. Are all the philosophical disputes among libertarians, such as the disagreements between defenders of natural rights and defenders of utilitarianism, absolutely necessary to the success of our movement? No, of course not. In most cases, our ability to convert others to our way of thinking has little if anything to do with technical matters of philosophy—though a basic philosophy, comprehensible to the masses, will always be indispensable. Likewise, early Christianity would have progressed (or not) even if theologians had never troubled themselves with fine points of theology.

So why did these internal battles erupt in the first place? Why didn't Christians simply follow and teach the general precepts of Jesus without developing a more comprehensive theology? One reason, I suggest, is that many church fathers were intellectuals with a serious interest in ideas and a good knowledge of various pagan philosophies. They wanted more than to preach and spread the doctrines of Christianity, which were really quite simple. They wanted to understand the philosophical implications of their religious beliefs, and to distinguish their beliefs from the many philosophical schools and ideas that were widespread in the Rome of their day.

The same reasoning applies to the modern libertarian movement. Many libertarians (including many nonacademics) are dedicated intellectuals with a strong desire to understand and develop the philosophical implications of individual freedom, quite apart from the irrelevance of those fine points in persuading others to join the libertarian cause. And, as was the case with early Christians, our intense interest in ideas has inevitably generated internal discord, as competing tribes of libertarian warriors have battled for their particular brand of libertarian theory.

All this is quite healthy, in my judgment. As I have said many times before, *internal dissent and debate make the libertarian movement an interesting place to be, even when it isn't moving anywhere.*

Most libertarians live *in* the movement, not merely with it. The movement—our conferences, periodicals, websites, e-lists, and so forth—constitute our intellectual home. Thus, however discouraging our lack of political progress may be over a period of time, the movement itself survives; and it will continue to survive so long as it remains intellectually vibrant. We value ideas about freedom not merely because we hope they will aid our quest for a free society. We also value ideas about freedom for their own sake, because of their inherent fascination. One can spend a lifetime investigating the ideas associated with freedom, as well as the strong appeal of freedom to a wide range of cultures across space and over time. And yet, as we approach the twilight of life, we may feel as though we have barely scratched the surface of this rich vein of thought. This is not mere speculation; it is based on my own experience.

Comparing the libertarian movement, which is still quite young, with the early Christian movement is not a stretch. How is it that a minority of Christians managed to survive and eventually prosper in a hostile social and political environment? And what, if anything, can libertarians learn from that success? The many differences between these movements are profound and, in the main, obvious. But an important similarity (discussed above) is not so obvious, namely the deep and lasting interest of both movements in ideas—an interest that extends far beyond the pragmatic value of those ideas—and the common commitment of both movements to an ideal. Both sought to develop a coherent, internally consistent system of ideas that impart meaning to life and make some things worth fighting for.

Unfortunately, within a few centuries, Christianity—which began as a pro-freedom movement in opposition to the Roman state and Roman culture—eventually allied itself with the state and substituted force for persuasion. Moreover, the Christian movement, unlike the libertarian movement, never acknowledged the supremacy of reason. Let us hope that the libertarian movement never replicates these momentous errors.

25

The Secularization of
Private Property

In the previous two chapters, I explained the traditional Christian view of property, according to which there existed only common property in the earliest societies, as illustrated in the biblical account of the Garden of Eden and in various Roman accounts of the Golden Age. Private property came about only after Adam's fall into sin had thoroughly corrupted human nature with avarice, pride, and other evil tendencies that were absent in prelapsarian man. God mandated private property (along with government and slavery) for postlapsarian man as a punishment and remedy for sin.

Here, I explore some features of secular accounts of the justification and origin of private property, especially as they appear after 1600 in the writings of various Protestant philosophers of natural law, most notably Hugo Grotius (1583–1645) and Samuel Pufendorf (1632–1694). To call these accounts "secular" is not to say that they omitted God from their accounts of natural law. Consider this famous passage by Grotius, from the Prolegomena to his celebrated and highly influential text, *The Rights of War and Peace* (1625): "What we have been saying [about natural law] would have a degree of validity even if we should concede that which cannot be conceded without the utmost wickedness, that there is no God, or that the affairs of men are of no concern to him."

Although Pufendorf and some other modern natural-law philosophers disagreed with Grotius in this matter, we should not suppose that Grotius was proposing an atheistic system of natural law. In fact, the position taken by Grotius had been around for many centuries, especially in the writings of Thomistic philosophers. Natural law, in the theory defended by Thomas Aquinas (1225–1274), is the part of divine law that is knowable to human reason without the aid of divine revelation, such as the Bible. Even God could not change the fundamental precepts of natural law, according to this approach, because doing so would require that God contradict himself, which is something that even omnipotence cannot do. God created human beings and their environment, and the basic precepts of natural law emerge necessarily from these elementary facts. True, God could have created man with a different nature than he now has; in that case, different natural-law principles might apply. But given human nature as God created it, the *fundamental* precepts of natural law are permanent and unchangeable, and every human being can know them through the use of reason.

In opposition to this *intellectualist* school of thought (as it is often called) stood the theory known as *voluntarism*—so called because of its emphasis on the primacy of God's will over his intellect. Voluntarism is often associated with Duns Scotus (1266–1308) and William of Ockham (1287–1347). In the voluntarist scheme, God's will is primary and literally can accomplish anything, including transforming something that is currently evil into something good, and vice versa. Consider the age-old question: *Is something good because God wills it, or does God will it because it is good?* The voluntarists embraced the first part of this dichotomy, claiming that actions are good or evil merely because God wills them to be so. Thus, if God were to will that rape and murder are morally good, then those actions would become morally good.

Aquinas and other intellectualists disagreed, of course. Even God could not render rape and murder morally good, given human nature as he created it. After creation, therefore,

God wills something because it is good; his willing, per se, does not make it so. Or, to speak more precisely, God's will necessarily coincides with the good, because having willed that humans should possess certain characteristics, he simultaneously willed the moral implications of those characteristics. The fundamental moral precepts of natural law could change only if human nature itself were to change.

We see traces of this approach in the theory of original sin and its influence on the Christian theory of property rights. Given human nature in its undefiled, prelapsarian state, common property was a precept of natural law. But original sin drastically *changed* human nature, so God mandated special institutions—namely, private property, government, and slavery—that overrode the original natural law; these institutions were needed to control and punish humans who had become vitiated with sin. (Some historians, most notably Ernst Troeltsch in his classic work, *The Social Teachings of the Christian Churches* [1911], have dubbed the divine commands for sinful human beings a *secondary natural law*, but there has been some controversy over whether that label is accurate. Rather, many theologians view those commands as a type of divine *positive* law, not as a species of natural law. Although I am personally fascinated by this and similar controversies within Christianity, I doubt if many of my readers, especially my fellow atheists, share my interest in such arcane theological disputes. I will therefore avoid detours into technical points as much as possible and rest content with generalizations.)

Returning to Grotius: he claimed that the precepts of natural law would remain valid even if there were no God. That places him squarely within the intellectualist tradition of Aquinas and others. Grotius also wrote in the Prolegomena, shortly after his notorious statement about God, "But the law of nature of which we have spoken, comprising alike that which relates to the social life of man and that which is so called in a larger sense, proceeding as it does from the essential traits implanted in man, can nevertheless rightly be attributed to God because of his having willed that such traits exist in us."

Thus, as noted earlier, the secular approach to property rights did not altogether exclude God from the picture. But the secular approach, generally speaking, rested its claims on reason and history, not on biblical authority and certainly not on papal decrees, as Catholic writers on natural law frequently did. Many secular philosophers of natural law, such as Grotius and John Locke, were liberal Protestants who rejected a literal reading of the Bible. Hence, Grotius regarded Adam as a general "type," not as a specific individual; Adam represents human beings before the evolution of private property. Likewise, the story of Cain and Abel—"a tiller of the ground" and "a keeper of sheep" respectively, according to Genesis 4:2—symbolizes an early division of labor that resulted in violent conflict. And the "tree of knowledge" from which Adam and Eve ate the forbidden fruit symbolizes a growing awareness of moral options, both good and evil, from which man must choose. Although Grotius agreed with conventional Christian teaching that mankind in his primitive state was probably morally innocent, he speculated that this innocence resulted from an ignorance of vice, not from a commitment to virtue. The vicious tendencies that many Christians attributed to original sin were, for Grotius, the consequence of the greater number of options and sources of pleasure that attended more advanced societies. With more choices and more appealing things to choose from came greater temptations. As a number of writers in the Grotian tradition would later observe, if there was virtually no theft in early, primitive societies, it was because they produced nothing worth stealing.

Moreover, there is no hint of original sin or its effects on human nature in the accounts of Grotius or other secular philosophers of that era. Although Grotius cited Genesis and other parts of the Bible from time to time, he treated them as historical sources, exactly as he did when citing Livy, Tacitus, Seneca, Cicero, and other pagan writers.

When it came to the issue of common and private owner-ship, the key passages were those found in the first chapter of Genesis, as in verse 26 (RSV):

> Then God said, "Let us make man in our image, after our likeness; and let them have dominion over the fish of the sea, and over the birds of the air, and over the cattle, and over all the earth, and over every creeping thing that creeps upon the earth."

Since God granted "dominion" over the earth and its non-human creatures to mankind in general, this decree became a pillar passage used to support the claim that prelapsarian man owned everything in common. (Sir Robert Filmer, John Locke's primary target in *Two Treatises of Government*, was a curious exception; Filmer maintained that God's grant of dominion over the earth was made to Adam as an individual, so private property was established at the outset.) For cen-turies, therefore, controversies over common versus private property hinged on the meaning of "dominion." Whatever we may think of the source of these controversies, the ensuing debates served a valuable role in clarifying the meanings of "common" and "private" property.

Some leading Protestant theorists of natural law made an important innovation in this field: they distinguished between a positive and a negative community of goods. In his massive and highly influential work on international law, *Of the Law of Nature and Nations*, Samuel Pufendorf wrote,

> It is clear that before any convention of men existed there was a community of all things, not, indeed, such as we have called positive, but a negative one, that is, that all things lay open to all men, and belonged no more to one than to another.[34]

In other words, in the primitive condition of mankind, all natural resources were *unowned*, and all people possessed an equal right to *use* those unowned goods. Grotius had previously defended this notion of a negative community of goods with equal-use rights, but his explanation was not as clear as that given by Pufendorf; and it was Pufendorf who first applied the terms "negative" and "positive" to this issue. A positive community of, say, land would have been akin to joint ownership, a condition in which *every* person would have a say in how land was used. It was this conception—as used, for example, by Herbert Spencer—that made private property in land (or any other natural resource) very difficult to justify. (See my discussion in "Herbert Spencer, Henry George, and the Land Question, Part 2."[35])

But the conception of a *negative* community of goods, as defended by Grotius, Pufendorf, and many other modern writers on natural law, was a different matter entirely. Here the common right was not one of joint ownership but of *usufruct*, or the equal right to use unowned property that had not already been appropriated by others for their use. A notion of private property was latent in this notion of a negative commons and a universal-use right, as Pufendorf pointed out:

> But since things are of no use to men unless at least their fruits may be appropriated, and this is impossible if others as well can take what we already by our own act selected for our uses, it follows that the first convention [about private property rights] between men was about these very concerns, to the effect that whatever one of these things which were left open to all, and of their fruits, a man had laid his hands upon, with intent to turn it to his uses, could not be taken from him by another.[36]

Grotius had made the same point. The primitive communism discussed by many ancient writers was not a type of joint ownership. Rather the common right in question was to the "*use* of all things," and this common-use right served the same purpose in primitive societies that private property would later serve in more advanced civilizations. Suppose I pick some apples from a tree with the intention of eating them. Prior to my action, every other person had an equal right to use those apples; but *after* I appropriate them it would be unjust for anyone to take those apples from me. At that point in time I may be said to have *dominion* over those apples. The fact that I must *consume* the apples in the course of using them, thereby leaving nothing behind for others to use, does not violate the rights of anyone else, for no one had property rights in the apples before I used them. Suppose, in contrast, that the apple tree was already the private property of another person. In that case, I would be committing theft if I picked the apples without the owner's permission.

According to Grotius, the fact that food and drink must be consumed in the very act of using them, thereby leaving nothing behind for others, implies the notion of private property. Over time, this notion was gradually extended to other resources. As Grotius explained in a very interesting passage in *Commentary on the Law of Prize and Booty*:

> It is evident . . . that the present-day concept of distinction in ownership was the result, not of any sudden transition, but of a gradual process whose initial

steps were taken under the guidance of nature herself. For there are some things which are consumed
by use, either in the sense that they are converted into
the very substance of the user and therefore admit of
no further use, or else in the sense that they are rendered less fit for additional service by the fact that
they have once been made to serve. Accordingly, it
very soon became apparent, in regard to articles of the
first class (for example, food and drink), that a certain
form of private ownership was inseparable from use.
For the essential characteristic of private property is
the fact that it belongs to a given individual in such
a way as to be incapable of belonging to any other
individual. This basic concept was later extended
by a logical process to include articles of the second
class, such as clothing and various other things capable of being moved or of moving themselves. Because
of these developments, it was not even possible for
all immovable things (fields, for instance) to remain
unapportioned, since the use of such things, while it
does not consist directly in their consumption, is nevertheless bound up [in some cases] with purposes of
consumption (as it is when arable lands and orchards

are used with a view to obtaining food, or pastures for [animals intended to provide] clothing), and since there are not enough immovable goods to suffice for indiscriminate use by all persons.[37]

Much more remains to be said about the secular conception of private property, and I continue the discussion in the next chapter.

26

Private Property and Natural Law

In previous chapters, I explained how the traditional Christian view of private property hinged on the deleterious effects of original sin on human nature. As Robert and Alexander Carlyle wrote in their magisterial six-volume work, *A History of Medieval Political Theory in the West*, the views expressed by Augustine (364–430) and Pope Gregory the Great (540–604) typified the approach of the Catholic Church for many centuries:

> Both St. Augustine and St. Gregory look upon the institution of coercive government as not belonging to the primitive state of man; they do not think that government of this kind is a natural institution; but

this does not mean that the Fathers look upon the ordered government of society among men as they actually are, as a thing improper or illegitimate. We have already, in considering their attitude to the institution of slavery, recognized that they conceive of the conditions proper to human life as having been completely altered by the entrance of sin into the world. Slavery was contrary to the natural law of the primitive condition of human innocence, but is proper and even useful under the actual conditions of human nature. It is the same with the institution of government. Coercive government has been made necessary through sin, and is a divinely appointed remedy for sin.[38]

As I described in the preceding chapters, private property was the third part of this trinity. If not for original sin, only common property would have been consistent with natural law; but with Adam's fall came the corruption of human nature with evil tendencies (primarily avarice, or greed). Thus, God mandated private property to deal with this new condition. Private property, by distinguishing mine from thine, established boundaries—specified and enforced by government—designed to keep avarice in check and to punish violators. This is essentially what Augustine meant when he said that private property was decreed by God as a remedy and punishment for sin. As Alexander Carlyle explained in "The Theory of Property in Medieval Theology," the Christian position led to the conclusion that private property is conventional, that it exists only by virtue of governmental laws and decisions:

These theories are intelligible only when brought into relation with that fundamental conception of the contrast between the natural and the conventional. . . . This view is the opposite of that of Locke, that private property is an institution of natural law, and arises out of labour. To the Fathers the only natural condition is that of common ownership and individual use. The world was made for the common benefit of mankind, that all should receive from it what they require. They admit, however, that human nature being what it is, greedy, avaricious, and vicious, it is impossible for men to live normally under the condition of common ownership. This represents the more perfect way of life, and this principle was represented in the organization of the monastic life, as it gradually took shape. For mankind in general, some organization of ownership became necessary, and this was provided by the State and its laws, which have decided the conditions and limitations of ownership. Private property is practically the creation of the State, and is defined, limited, and changed by the State.[39]

The natural-law theory of private property, as defended by John Locke and many other classical liberals, took many centuries to emerge. Some changes began to appear in the later Middle Ages. The intense interest in Roman law—the so-called "reception" that began to take off in the 11th century—and the largely spontaneous development of feudal law played important roles, as did the rediscovery of Aristotle's works, beginning in the mid-12th century. Some church authorities reacted negatively to any effort to Christianize Aristotle, given how his naturalistic viewpoint conflicted with Christian beliefs. Among the dangers were Aristotle's teachings that the universe has existed eternally, his denial of the personal immortality of the soul, and his implicit rejection of miracles, which followed from the Aristotelian doctrine that natural causation is everywhere operative.

Nevertheless, these obstacles were eventually overcome, thanks primarily to Thomas Aquinas and his grand synthesis, the *Summa Theologica*, which adroitly combined Christianity and the general perspective of "the Philosopher." This synthesis was a significant innovation for the time, but as the Christian version of Aristotle became a pillar of orthodoxy, it retarded some aspects of scientific progress. (This negative influence should not be exaggerated. The primary problem with Aristotle was in the field of physics; his influence was largely beneficial in biology and botany.)

There was nothing resembling original sin in the writings of Aristotle, and his conception of the "natural" differed from the traditional Christian conception. For Aristotle, "natural" did not signify an original, or primitive, condition, as we find in the theory of a Golden Age defended by Stoics and Christians; rather, "natural" signified the goal-directed development of an entity or social state into a more perfect, fully developed condition, as when an acorn grows into an oak tree. As Walter Ullmann noted in *Medieval Political Thought* (1975), this was a dramatic shift from the traditional Christian view:

> Aristotle's thought was pervaded by the idea of nature as the driving force, which was conceived in teleological terms: "Nature does nothing superfluous," or "Nature behaves as if it foresaw the future," or "Nature does nothing in vain," were some of his often recurring statements which, with their strong teleological

bias, could hardly fail to fall on receptive ears—and yet, what a difference there was between his and the traditional theology: the laws of nature determined man's thinking and reasoning capacity. The hallmark of man was the employment of his will and reason by which the laws of nature were expressed.

The upshot of Aristotle's social doctrines was that the state, private property, and slavery were natural institutions that developed over time to serve the rational purposes of human beings. In adopting similar positions about those institutions, Aquinas typically cited Aristotle (especially the *Politics*) as his source. Consider Aquinas's defense of slavery in his *Summa Theologica*: "Slavery among men is natural, for some men are naturally slaves, as the Philosopher proves at *Politics* I." And again,

> The fact that this man is a slave rather than that [man] is due not to the nature of the man considered simply as such, but to some advantage consequent upon his being so, in that it is beneficial for a slave to be governed by someone wiser than he, and for a master to be assisted by the slave, as the Philosopher says at *Politics* I.

Likewise, when reviewing the nature and justification of
the state (conceived in this context as an organized political
community governed by laws, not merely as a ruling body, or
"government" in the narrow sense), Aquinas again embraced
the perspective of Aristotle, in part if not in total. The state
is not a deviation from the original natural law, as earlier
theologians had claimed. Aquinas agreed with the traditional
view that a coercive government would have been unnecessary in man's innocent, prelapsarian condition; nevertheless,
he maintained that the state is "natural" in the sense that
it is based on human nature, is justified by human reason,
and is essential for men to achieve their full potential as
human beings.

Lastly, as expected, Aquinas justified private property along
the same lines, again citing Aristotle as his chief authority.
Consider Aquinas's reply to the argument that Christians
should reject private property as contrary to natural law
because common property was the original condition of mankind before Adam's fall into sin:

> Community of goods is attributed to the natural
> law not because natural right dictates that all things
> should be possessed in common and that nothing
> should be possessed as one's own, but because the

> division of possessions is not according to natural
> right, but, rather, according to human agreement,
> which belongs to positive right. . . . Hence the own-
> ership of possessions is not contrary to natural right;
> rather, it is an addition to natural right devised by
> human reason.

That view is still a long way from Locke's argument that
private property is a natural right originally based on labor.
But Aquinas moved closer to the modern liberal view that
private property advances a *positive* social good and is not
merely a remedial and punitive institution mandated by God
for sinful human beings. The essential role played by private
property in maintaining peaceful social cooperation is a dis-
covery of human reason, so private property is "natural" in
that sense. Reason has supplemented the original natural law,
not contradicted it.

Before concluding this chapter, I want to make an important
observation about the status of private property in emergency
situations, as when a man would starve if he did not steal food
from another person. From the early church fathers through
the Middle Ages and well into the modern era, it was argued
that a man in dire need has a *right* to the property of those
people who possess more property than they reasonably need.

This was seen as a positive, enforceable right, not merely as a moral mandate for voluntary charity. Strictly speaking, if a starving man absconded with food that belonged to a wealthy man, he was not "stealing" at all; he was simply taking that which belonged to him by right.

Although this right found in emergency scenarios was justified in various ways, it was closely linked to the premise that God originally gave the earth and its resources to mankind in common for the benefit of all. Christian theologians, early and late, unanimously argued that a surplus of private property (i.e., more property than is needed to satisfy one's basic needs) is justifiable only if such property is used for the common good. As Aquinas put it, "man ought to hold external things not as his own, but as common: that is, in such a way that he is ready to share them with others in the event of need." Human need trumps private property rights in emergency situations; so, as Aquinas explained, for a starving man to take food from a rich man, even without the permission of the latter, does not qualify as an unjust act at all.

> If . . . there is a necessity so urgent and clear that it is obvious that the necessity must be met at once by whatever means are to hand—for example, if a person is in immediate danger and no other help is

available—anyone can then lawfully supply his own need from the property of another by taking from it either openly or in secret; nor, properly speaking, does this have the character of theft or robbery.

This doctrine survived even in the writings of leading Protestant natural-law philosophers during the 17th century, whose overall approach tended to be more secular than that of their Catholic counterparts. For example, when Hugo Grotius defended this emergency right, he added that, if necessity compelled him to take the property of another person, "I certainly ought to make that Man Restitution as soon as I am able to do it." This position on restitution was later criticized by Samuel Pufendorf, who correctly pointed out that one cannot legitimately demand restitution from a person in need if that person is merely exercising his natural right to appropriate and use the property of others. Where no injustice had been committed, no restitution is required.

Oddly, perhaps, the same emergency right was defended by John Locke in his *First Treatise of Government*: "*Charity* gives every man a Title to so much out of another's Plenty, as will keep him from extreme want, where he has no means to subsist otherwise." In using the word "Title," Locke made it clear that he was speaking not merely of a moral obligation to be charitable but of a *positive right enforceable by govern-ment.* Early defenders of this right almost always applied it narrowly to life-or-death situations. But later defenders of the welfare state easily adapted the same premise to justify their schemes for the extensive redistribution of private property by governments.

27

John Locke on Property

In *On the Law of Nature and Nations*, Samuel Pufendorf (one of the most influential modern philosophers of law) drew a crucial distinction between two possible meanings of a "community of goods."

> The term *community* is taken either *negatively* or *positively*. In the former case things are said to be common, according as they are considered before the interposition of any human act, as a result of which they are held to belong in a special way to this man rather than to that. In the same sense such things are said to be nobody's more in a negative than in a positive sense; that is, that they are not yet assigned to a particular person, not that they cannot be assigned to a particular person. They are, furthermore, called

"things that lie open to any and every person." But common things, by the second and positive meaning, differ from things owned, only in the respect that the latter belong to one person while the former belong to several in the same manner.[40]

The distinction drawn by Pufendorf—and by Hugo Grotius before him, if in a less explicit manner—is fraught with momentous implications. If, before the advent of private property, the earth and its resources were common in a negative sense, then such resources were simply unowned and everyone had a right to use them for his or her own benefit. But if the earth and its resources were common in a positive sense, then we had a primitive condition of *joint ownership*, and that would have required the unanimous consent of *all* the owners before any individual could legitimately appropriate property for his or her own use.

John Locke's position on the primitive condition of common dominion has engendered a fair amount of scholarly controversy. Locke, like every Christian philosopher before him, accepted as authoritative two key passages in the first chapter of Genesis, verses 26 and 28. Here is verse 26 (RSV).

Then God said, "Let us make man in our image, after our likeness; and let them have dominion over the fish of the sea, over the birds of the air, and over the cattle, and over all the earth, and over every creeping thing that creeps on the earth."

According to Sir Robert Filmer, Locke's target in the *First Treatise of Government*, the grant of dominion was bestowed on Adam as an individual. By virtue of that divine authorization, Adam became owner of the entire earth and its resources, after which title passed from Adam to his eldest male heirs. And since ownership of land entails political dominion, according to Filmer, Adam was also appointed by God as absolute monarch over the entire world—a power that was passed to his rightful heirs, as determined by the principle of primogeniture.

Locke had little trouble disposing of Filmer's tortuous arguments for the divine right of kings, which was a relatively modern doctrine. Earlier Christians had typically maintained that *government* is a divinely mandated institution but had not gone so far as to claim that *specific individuals* were appointed by God to rule over others. (Many Catholic philosophers during the High Middle Ages invoked some version of consent theory.) However, that was precisely the position defended by Filmer and other proponents of the divine right of kings. And that position, in turn, became the foundation not only for modern absolutism, but also for the common claim of absolutists that kings were the legitimate owners of all land in their kingdoms. Thus, when a king confiscated land from his subjects, or when he claimed absolute political sovereignty over inhabitants of that land, he was simply exercising his rights as a legitimate owner, an ownership originally bestowed by God on Adam.

Although Filmer had died decades before Locke wrote his refutation, Filmer's tracts were printed around 1680 to buttress the absolutist claims of Charles II and the Stuart dynasty generally. This background helps explain the contemporary significance of Locke's *First Treatise*, even though much of it may strike the modern reader as tedious and irrelevant. Locke was not the only individualist of his time to take on Filmer; similar criticisms were written by Locke's friend James Tyrrell (in *Patriarcha non Monarcha)* and by Algernon Sidney (in *Discourses Concerning Government*). The critiques by three leading individualists of the 17th century testify to Filmer's importance at the time.

Contrary to Filmer, Locke maintained that the passages in Genesis should be understood as a grant of dominion not to Adam in particular, but to mankind in general. (He pointed out, for example, that Genesis says "let *them* have dominion," not "him.") But what exactly did that mean? Did Locke accept the negative or the positive view of common property, as outlined by Pufendorf? Did he embrace the negative view of a community of goods, according to which the earth and its resources were originally *unowned* and that every person had an equal right to *use* those unowned resources, or did he believe that the earth and its resources were jointly owned in a positive sense by every person?

Modern scholars have disagreed in their interpretations of Locke, which is understandable, given that Locke never expressly took a stand on the issue. The most reasonable interpretation, in my judgment, is that Locke agreed with Pufendorf's "negative" understanding of the commons, before the advent of private property. This interpretation of Locke, according to which natural resources were originally unowned rather than jointly owned, was advanced by two early Lockeans: Jean Barbeyrac (1674–1744), a French philosopher and a translator of Pufendorf, and Gershom Carmichael (1672–1729), a seminal figure in the early Scottish Enlightenment who brought a Lockean perspective to bear in his commentaries on Pufendorf.

Some modern Lockean scholars have also defended the negative interpretation. I especially recommend the detailed analysis by Martin Seliger in *The Liberal Politics of John Locke* (Praeger, 1968), and the treatment by Stephen Buckle in his superb book *Natural Law and the Theory of Property*: *Grotius to Hume.* Buckle summarized Locke's position as follows:

> The world is given to mankind in common in such a way that it initially belongs to no one in particular—the original meaning of "common" identified by Grotius, and termed negative community by Pufendorf. Locke insists that the world has been given in common in order to reject Filmer's doctrine that the world is the private property of Adam and his heirs. . . .[41]

Since many readers of this volume may not be especially interested in a rather technical issue—namely, the distinction between a negative and positive understanding of the primitive commons—I want to highlight the theoretical significance of this controversy. Suppose, on the one hand, that we accept the negative interpretation, according to which natural resources were originally unowned. In that case, the justification of private property is not especially difficult. But suppose, on the other hand, that we accept the positive interpretation, according to which natural resources were originally jointly owned. In that case, private property is quite difficult to justify, since the private appropriation of natural resources would require the consent of all the commoners.

Locke was undoubtedly aware of Pufendorf's distinction between negative and positive commons, since he praised Pufendorf's work as the best book of its kind. And there are some important similarities between the two writers. Consider again this passage from Pufendorf's *On the Law of Nature and Nations*, which I quoted in chapter 25. After explaining the negative commons to be a situation before the emergence of private property in which "all things lay open to all men, and belonged no more to one than to another," Pufendorf continued,

> But since things are of no use to men unless at least their fruits may be appropriated, and this is impossible if others as well can take what we have already by our own act selected for our uses, it follows that the first convention between men was about these very concerns, to the effect that whatever one of these things which were left open to all, and of their fruits, a man had laid his hands upon, with intent to turn it to his uses, could not be taken from him by another.[42]

Although Locke agreed that natural resources would be useless unless they could be appropriated for private use, he disagreed with Pufendorf's emphasis on convention, or consent, as necessary to the establishment of private property.

Indeed, in chapter 5 of the *Second Treatise of Government*, "Of Property," Locke stated his intention to show "how Men come to have a *property* in several parts of that which God gave to Mankind in common, and that without any express Compact of all the Commoners." The justification of private property, according to Locke, "does not depend on the express consent of all the Commoners." (This position alone indicates that Locke's view of the original commons was negative, not positive. There are other indicators as well.)

Attentive readers may have noticed that Locke specifically excluded the *express* consent of the commoners as a necessary condition of private property. Both Grotius and Pufendorf had specified that the necessary consent may be either *implied or express*, so Locke's disagreement with his two predecessors may not have been so serious after all. Locke did assign some role for implied consent in his theory of property, but this is one of those matters that is too troublesome and technical to discuss here. For now, suffice it to say that Locke did not regard the consent of the commoners, whether express or implied, as essential to the *moral justification* of private property.

Notes

[1] George H. Smith, "The Righteous Persecution of Drug Consumers," chap. 12 in *Atheism, Ayn Rand, and Other Heresies* (Amherst, NY: Prometheus Books, 1990).

[2] Walter Ullmann, *The Individual and Society in the Middle Ages* (Baltimore, MD: Johns Hopkins, 1966), p. 37.

[3] R. W. Southern, *Western Society and the Church in the Middle Ages* (London: Penguin Books, 1970), p. 17.

[4] Quoted in G. G. Coulton, *Inquisition and Liberty* (Boston: Beacon Press, 1959), pp. 103–4.

[5] Southern, *Western Society*, p. 17.

[6] Bernard Hamilton, *The Medieval Inquisition* (New York: Holmes & Meier Publishers, Inc., 1981), p. 25. Quote in R. I., *The Formation of a Persecuting Society: Authority and Deviance in Western Europe, 950–1250*, 2nd ed. (Oxford: Blackwell Publishing, 2007), p. 100.

[7] Quotations from Martin Luther, *Secular Authority* [1523], in John Dillenberger, ed., *Martin Luther: Selections from His Writings* (New York: Anchor Books, 1961), pp. 363–402.

[8] Ibid.

[9] Ibid.

[10] Roland Bainton, *Hunted Heretic: The Life and Death of Michael Servetus, 1511–1553* (Beacon Press, 1953).

[11] Pierre Bayle, et al., *The Dictionary Historical and Critical of Mr. Peter Bayle, vol. 5* (London: 1738), p. 482.

[12] Ibid.

[13] Ibid., p. 483.

[14] J. M. Robertson, *The Dynamics of Religion*, 2nd ed. (London: Watts & Co., 1926), pp. 65–66.

[15] George H. Smith, "Thomas Paine Versus Edmund Burke, Part 2," Libertarianism.org, May 2, 2014.

[16] Leonard W. Levy, *Blasphemy: Verbal Offense against the Sacred, from Moses to Salman Rushdie* (New York: Knopf, 1993), p. 346.

[17] Leonard W. Levy, *Blasphemy: Verbal Offense Against the Sacred, from Moses to Salman Rushdie* (Chapel Hill: University of North Carolina Press Books, 1995), p. 398.

[18] For a brilliant account of the impact of Pyrrhonic skepticism on modern philosophy, see Richard H. Popkin, *The History of Scepticism from Erasmus to Descartes*, rev. ed. (New York: Harper and Row, 1964).

[19] Jonathan Israel, *Radical Enlightenment* (Oxford, UK: Oxford University Press, 2001).

[20] Jonathan Israel, *Enlightenment Contested* (Oxford, UK: Oxford University Press, 2006).

[21] Ibid., p. 36.

[22] Baruch Spinoza, *A Theologico-Political Treatise* (1670), p. 124.

[23] George H. Smith, "The Philosophy of the Declaration of Independence, Part 2," Libertarianism.org, November 29, 2011.

[24] Jean Meslier, *Testament: Memoir of the Thoughts and Sentiments of Jean Meslier*, trans. Michael Shreve (Amherst, NY: Prometheus Books, 2009).

[25] Michael Onfray, "Jean Meslier and 'The Gentle Inclination of Nature,'" *New Politics* X, No. 4 (2006): 1–29.

[26] Ibid.

[27] Paul Eltzbacher, *The Great Anarchists: Ideas and Teachings of Seven Major Thinkers* (Mineola, NY: Dover Publications, 2004), p. 292.

[28] Alexander J. Carlyle, "The Theory of Property in Medieval Theology," in *Property: Its Duties and Rights* (London: Macmillan, 1922), p. 132.

[29] Ibid. p. 151.

[30] Christopher Hill, *The World Turned Upside Down: Radical Ideas during the English Revolution* (New York: Viking Press, 1973), p. 133.

[31] Ludwig von Mises, *Socialism: An Economic and Sociological Analysis*, trans. J. Kahane (Indianapolis, IN: Liberty Fund, 1981), pp. 41–42.

[32] Seneca, "Letter XC," in *Seneca: Letters from a Stoic*, trans. Robin Campbell (Penguin Books, 2004), 174.

[33] Ibid., pp. 174–75.

[34] Samuel Pufendorf, *Of the Law of Nature and Nations* [1672], trans. C. H. Oldfather and W. A. Oldfather (Oxford, UK: Clarendon Press, 1934), p. 537.

[35] George H. Smith, "Herbert Spencer, Henry George, and the Land Question, Part 2," Libertarianism.org, July 9, 2013.

[36] Pufendorf, *Of the Law of Nature and Nations*, p. 537.

[37] Hugo Grotius, *Commentary on the Law of Prize and Booty* [1603], trans. Gwladys L. Williams (Indianapolis, IN: Liberty Fund, 2006), pp. 317–18 (brackets in the original).

[38] Robert W. Carlyle and Alexander J. Carlyle, *A History of Medieval Political Theory in the West*, vol. I [1903] (Edinburgh: Blackwood, 1950), p. 123.

[39] Alexander J. Carlyle, "The Theory of Property in Medieval Theology," in Gore & Hobhouse, eds., *Property: Its Duties and Rights* (London: Macmillan, 1913).

[40] Pufendorf, *Of the Law of Nature and Nations*, p. 532.

[41] Stephen Buckle, *Natural Law and the Theory of Property: Grotius to Hume* (Oxford, UK: Clarendon Press, 1991), p. 175.

[42] Pufendorf, *Of the Law of Nature and Nations*, p. 537.

Index

Libertarianism.org

Liberty. It's a simple idea and the linchpin of a complex system of values and practices: justice, prosperity, responsibility, toleration, cooperation, and peace. Many people believe that liberty is the core political value of modern civilization itself, the one that gives substance and form to all the other values of social life. They're called libertarians.

Libertarianism.org is the Cato Institute's treasury of resources about the theory and history of liberty. The book you're holding is a small part of what Libertarianism.org has to offer. In addition to hosting classic texts by historical libertarian figures and original articles from modern-day thinkers, Libertarianism.org publishes podcasts, videos, online introductory courses, and books on a variety of topics within the libertarian tradition.

Cato Institute

Founded in 1977, the Cato Institute is a public policy research foundation dedicated to broadening the parameters of policy debate to allow consideration of more options that are consistent with the principles of limited government, individual liberty, and peace. To that end, the Institute strives to achieve greater involvement of the intelligent, concerned lay public in questions of policy and the proper role of government.

The Institute is named for *Cato's Letters*, libertarian pamphlets that were widely read in the American Colonies in the early 18th century and played a major role in laying the philosophical foundation for the American Revolution.

Despite the achievement of the nation's Founders, today virtually no aspect of life is free from government encroachment. A pervasive intolerance for individual rights is shown by government's arbitrary intrusions into private economic transactions and its disregard for civil liberties. And while freedom around the globe has notably increased in the past several decades, many countries have moved in the opposite direction, and most governments still do not respect or safeguard the wide range of civil and economic liberties.

To address those issues, the Cato Institute undertakes an extensive publications program on the complete spectrum of policy issues. Books, monographs, and shorter studies are commissioned to examine the federal budget, Social Security, regulation, military spending, international trade, and myriad other issues. Major policy conferences are held throughout the year, from which papers are published thrice yearly in the *Cato Journal*. The Institute also publishes the quarterly magazine *Regulation*.

In order to maintain its independence, the Cato Institute accepts no government funding. Contributions are received from foundations, corporations, and individuals, and other revenue is generated from the sale of publications. The Institute is a nonprofit, tax-exempt, educational foundation under Section 501(c)3 of the Internal Revenue Code.

CATO INSTITUTE
1000 Massachusetts Ave., N.W.
Washington, D.C. 20001
www.cato.org

CPSIA information can be obtained
at www.ICGtesting.com
Printed in the USA
FSOW01n2121161017
39992FS